Personality Types

JANE JOHN-NWANKWO RN, MSN

Personality Types

Copyright © 2014 by Jane John-Nwankwo.

ISBN-13: 978-1502579270

ISBN-10: 1502579278

Printed in the United States of America

www.janejohn-nwankwo.com
www.djngbooks.org

www.janejohn-nwankwo.com

www.djngbooks.org

"And above all, have fervent love for one another: for love shall cover the multitude of sins."
– 1 Peter 4:8

OTHER TITLES FROM THE SAME AUTHOR:

Personality Types

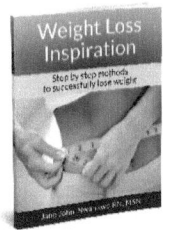

We can all live together if

we pause to understand

each other's personalities

-Jane John-Nwankwo

Chapter 1
ISTJ - The Duty Fulfiller

The ISTJ personality is the abbreviated form of Introversion, Sensing, Thinking and Judgment type of personality which covers approximately 10-14% of the world's population. This kind of personality is a combination of traits which offers positive values; but to others, it has some negative effects.

Below is a breakdown of attributes innate of the ISTJ, which others have aptly summed up as the duty fulfiller among personalities.

- *Quiet and Reserved* – They love security and peaceful environments. Noisy communities are what they would always stay away from as opting for a quiet kind of life is included in their goals.

  They would opt to being alone or together with a few friends with whom they have close relationships with rather than stay in a sea of people who may not share the same sentiments as they do. This is their way of showing that introversion is alive and well inside their system.

- *Intense Sense of Duty* – These are people who work longer hours to finish a task they deem as with high importance or worth fulfilling. They are highly motivated and geared to do all tasks that were placed on them. They have more appreciation not only on their achievements but on how they were able to surpass obstacles that stood in the way of fulfilling tasks.

- *Organized and Systematic* – Generally, these people succeed in their endeavors as they use a systematic approach which makes them waste no time in trying to go over their assigned work. Their homes are fully maintained and well-appointed. They believe in doing things in accordance to procedures or previously set guidelines.

- *Loyal and Dependable* – Being loyal and sincere towards their jobs, people see them as dependable persons. Honesty and integrity play major roles in their lives. They put more effort in doing things the right way and seeing things through as they have previously promised. They put more effort in meeting deadlines which makes people rely more on them than other personality types.

- *Possess Offbeat Sense of Humor* – As they are serious individuals, this characteristic does not make them good at cracking jokes. They would usually introduce jokes that not all may find funny but it would seem fun during gatherings.

This means, they may appear interesting individuals as they try their best at mingling even if they are not commonly used to bigger groups.

- *Responsible* – The preference of working alone is always there but being open to working with other individuals is there as well; most especially if a project or situation requires it. These are persons who like to take responsibility for their actions and decisions whether it involves family, work or relationships.

ISTJs take parenting seriously and family, to them, it is their reason for working hard. Apparently, they also enjoy being the person in authority that is why they do things to the best of their ability.

- *Internally-focused* - People who go by this trait depend on their five senses and deal with facts in a concrete fashion. In short—they employ the logical approach.

They seem not to be bothered by what the big picture is as they believe in dealing with facts and future possibilities. Their sensing attribute makes them do away with the abstract.

Weaknesses of the ISTJ

ISTJs may tend to be obsessed with regards to the structure of ideas which makes them favor doing things by the book. They may appear as know-it-all type of persons; thus, this merits them more work than other coworkers. These people find refusing an assignment a hard task and in a lot of ways, people take advantage of them. You can just imagine seeing them performing their jobs using longer hours with most of the tasks piled on their tables.

They may prefer working alone than with a team although when a task warrants collaboration with others, they would easily agree without question. Duty fulfillers find it difficult to understand ideas or thinking that do not coincide with their own outlook and can be judgmental in a lot of ways. Nevertheless, if the idea was provided by somebody they have high regard of, then, that idea will be processed as a fact.

An ISTJ may find his feelings not attuned with the others'. Sometimes, they take other people's emotions for granted in their effort of doing things perfectly. A touch or pat on the back, which means a lot to others could be forgotten as a gesture which proves essential within the workplace. They feel that expressing emotions to other people is an uncomfortable thing to do.

What they are more into is expressing what they feel through the way they act; to them, no words are enough to soothe, show affection or alleviate stressful situations. These reservations are eventually overcome once they see the real picture as they are individuals who will use more effort in order to fill a need.

Another problem that may affect ISTJs is their tendency to succumb to a catastrophe mode as they are wary of the possibilities when it comes to outcomes. When this happens, they would blame themselves and feel depressed as to what they haven't done in the first place.

Lastly, in their effort of organizing their lives, people may see them as stingy. The reason for this is clear and that is to save money for their future use and in order for them to live a life they have dreamed from the start.

Careers Ideal for the Duty Fulfiller

An ISTJ learn best by choosing subjects he thinks are useful and practical; therefore, he may fit in many jobs. These task-oriented individuals may not enjoy materials that may seem too easy because these lead them to be doubtful of the outcome. There seems to be ease in managing the difference between work and play.

Their four main characteristics enable them to land on good jobs and these are very rewarding for them in the end. But what really makes them stand out from the others is their perseverance which is the best quality duty fulfillers have. Careers for duty fulfillers are abundant. Here are jobs they would possibly land on:

Business:
- Office Manager or Supervisor
- Auditor
- Accountant
- Efficiency Analyst
- Insurance Underwriter
- Logistics and Supply Manager
- Chief Information Officer
- Work Processing Expert

- Regulatory Compliance Officer

Sales or Service:
- Detective or Police Officer
- Military Officer
- Government Employee
- IRS Agent
- Sports and Equipment
- Real Estate Agent
- Merchandise Sales
- Corrections Sergeant/Officer

Finance:
- Stockbroker
- Investment Securities Officer
- Tax Examiner
- Credit Analyst
- Estate Planner
- Budget Analyst

Education:
- Librarian
- School Principal or Administrator
- Teacher specializing in Technical, Physical Education, Industrial or Mathematics

Legal and Technical:
- Legal   Secretary/paralegal worker

- Law Researcher
- Technical Writer
- Computer Programmer
- EEG Technologist
- Geologist
- Meteorologist
- Pharmaceutical Sales Person or Researcher
- Electrician
- Engineer: Mechanical, Industrial or Electrical
- Mechanic (vehicles)
- Airline Mechanic
- Agricultural Scientist

Health Care:
- Surgeon or Primary Care physician
- Dentist
- Veterinarian
- Nursing Administrator
- Health Care Administrator
- Medical Researcher
- Pharmacist or Pharmacy Technician
- Exercise Physiologist
- Biomedical or Laboratory Technologist

Overall, individuals like ISTJs use logical and reasonable approaches in dealing with everyday life and work and are extremely effective in achieving their pursuit of work excellence and peaceful life. They are best when working together or have ties with fellow ISTJs, ESTJs and even ISFPs or ESFP personalities.

Chapter 2

ISTP - The Mechanic

The ISTP or the Mechanic has many things in common with people belonging to other types of personalities. They may be reserved and quiet but highly curious on how and why things operate or work. Being referred to as the "mechanic" may have stemmed from their skills at mechanical things.

ISTP Characteristics

Characteristics of this personality vary just like the other types. Its main components are Introversion, Sensing, Thinking and Perception. Other descriptions of individuals who are found to have this type of personality are:

- Risk takers
- They got simple desires
- Interested in extreme sports
- Loyal towards their peers
- Possess sincere values
- Solve problems using the analytical way
- Get things done even if it means disregarding rules or laws

Complex Personality

14

This type of personality is among the most complex as described in the Jungian types of characters. The evidence lies in their seamless transformation from being quiet spectators to active participants or leaders, then back again into being invisible introverts.

Meaning, they have an on and off character trait and there is nothing in the middle. Spectators might be taken aback when suddenly a morose-looking individual transforms into an animated and energetic one who decides based on logic than using feelings.

Normally, it is hard to detect this type of person as besides being independent and self-contained, they are enigmatic. They would only choose to reveal depending on what they want to let other people know and when they deem the proper time to open up is.

Their hyperactive state of mind which to others may seem to be unguarded is actually more controlled in such a way that they know what they are getting into. However this abrupt change of character may be new to bystanders as what they would see is a 360 degree turnabout from these normally reserved individuals.

Crisis and Independence
They are found to be excellent when reacting in times of problems; a quality not found in other personalities. Using little time in preparing for a solution, this always elicits surprise from onlookers or other players of the game or situations.

At the most, they will continue to thrive until the crisis is over. They may be viewed as aloof or distant due to not fully engaging with other people and not fully sold out to social mores. The way they observe things are remarkable which they use in adapting known rules into practical application.

Their tremendous independence creates a sense of being self-sufficient. The confidence that sprouts from this positive quality enables them to be direct and abrupt at times that they speak literally without showing little or no concern of the outcome at all. They favor being left alone to do their thing and not happy being under other people's control just the way they would towards others.

Classroom Learning and Thrill-Seeking Attitudes

The normal classroom learning attitude of ISTPs is quite different from that of other individuals. While others find classroom learning as a normal setting, the "mechanics" may have difficulty in dealing with it. They believe that this type of setting is not a gauge for their intelligence. Being skeptical of what is being put in front of them is a natural reaction.

Nevertheless, ISTPs become energized by the thought of being introduced to new skills in sports like those that enable them to dwell on the extreme. Their energy towards thrilling experiences is a no-nonsense reality and these bursts of energy are responses to the stimuli mainly geared on the thrill stimuli. The mysterious troubleshooting ability is highly influenced by the combination of thrill and emotions.

Relationships

1. *As Lovers*: Commitment within a relationship is a far-fetched idea for most ISTPs as they would want to savor what they have at the moment rather than committing themselves seriously. Long term commitment will be put on hold for the time being but the possibility of seeing a relationship through until such a time is a rewarding idea for their partners.

   They have the ability to nurture romantic ties in order to create a stronger bond and a healthy one at that. But in times when interest towards their partner comes as a result of negligence on either part, the tendency to sulk is out of the question because they have the ability to move on fast.

2. *As Parents*: ISTPs are flexible when it comes to parenting and hate to use control over their brood. The breathing room they provide their children may have come from their own quality of not wanting to be under other peoples' control as well. But whenever discipline is needed they are quick at administering it.

   Influencing their own children's decision in life is not a goal for ISTPs. As they are able to maintain a distance between them and their offspring, they may also want to enjoy spending bonding time most especially done outdoors like fishing, hunting, hiking, boating and the like. They think of this type of bonding as a way to know the young members of the family better.

3. *On Friendships*: They use a child-like approach towards friendship and that makes them attractive although they may seem introverted to others. Many people are able to conclude that they make valuable friends and trusted confidantes. However, they choose who they go out with, like they look at similarities in hobbies or pastimes.

   Unless there is something common with what they do, they would see other people as uninteresting. Extroverts are welcome as the talkative nature boosts what's lacking in them; but to some extent, they will get tired of the bubbly nature of extroverts.

4. *At Work*: ISTPs can provide challenges in teams; they would be in a quandary of sorts at the onset of every team endeavor either heavily participating or merely observing at what is happening around them.

   Conversations that offer no value for what they see as purpose are not tolerated by ISTP individuals. They see this as a waste of time and might trigger them to leave an occasion or event. But once their interest is fueled up by some factors, this enables them to work using all stored knowledge and facts that have been inside their brains for quite a time.

Strengths and Weaknesses

Strengths and weaknesses in individuals are a natural thing since no one was born perfect. These negative and positive qualities make or break ISTP individuals and can guide others on how to deal with them. Below are the good and bad sides of the "mechanics".

Positive Factors

- Self-confidence
- Good listeners
- Fun to be with
- Optimistic
- Handle daily concerns realistically
- Resilience
- Respectful towards others' privacy
- Able to come up with projects that provide tangible results
- Independence

Negative Factors
- Finds difficulty in long term relationships
- Fall short of expressing emotions and feelings and tend to be insensitive towards others
- Their privacy goes beyond other's expectations and hates people who invade their own space
- Passion for excitement may stir others
- Working under strict regulations or supervised by incompetent people

Careers for ISTP Individuals

These are individuals who have varied interests when it comes to a lot of things and when it comes to careers, they may or may not be good at the major ones. Nevertheless, they would prove to be excellent in fields they are heavily interested in; given the right amount of autonomy. Below are some suggestions on which career is best and which would not provide some good outcome considering their work attitudes and own outlook.

Career Suggestions
- Detective
- Firefighter
- Astronaut
- Electrician or Mechanic
- Engineer
- Automotive Technician
- Industrial Engineer
- Rescue Team Member
- Sports journalist
- Athlete
- Small Entrepreneur
- Sketch Artist
- Biotechnology
- Pilot
- Mathematician
- Career in extreme sports or stunt
- Video Game Designer
- Computer Technician
- Computer Animator
- Software Developer
- Systems Analyst
- Data Analyst

This list does not limit the capacity of ISTPs but may serve merely as guides in order to maximize their true potentials. They may have areas of growth which when given time for enhancement can push ISTPs more to become successful in their field of endeavor.

What needs to be done:

- Push them to further motivate them into fulfilling their goals
- Help them to open up to see the bigger picture of things
- Enhance a more open communication with other individuals

Nonetheless, they can be good partners with the following personalities: Fellow ISTPs, ESTPs, ISFJs and ESFJs.

Chapter 3
ISFJ - The Nurturer

This type of personality is similar to the duty fulfiller when it comes to love for peace and harmony and the opposite of the mechanic when it comes to ability to feel for others. This may be a combination which could be ideal for a lot of people.

Nonetheless, there are still weaknesses that some individuals belonging to this group may find hard to change but thinking about upgrading one's personality in order to leap into a better one may not be a difficult thing to do after all. If there are words that better describe the ISFJ, they are: Dedication, Warmth and Sensitivity besides being normally described as owning Introversion, Sensing, Feeling and Judging qualities.

Habits Inherent of an ISFJ

The main characteristics ISFJs possess are the ability of being practical and stable, kind and conscientious and above all—reliability when it comes to follow through. Nurturers care deeply towards other individuals and most of the time they are concerned on providing happiness.

Perception
They have a high sense of perception and their interest in serving people comes from their advanced sense of observations on those who surround them.

They have the ability to store inside their minds all impressions they obtain from events or situations and recalling them with precision is easy. Simply put, they are quick to note if someone told a different story in contrast to what they have professed previously by looking at some discrepancies in details and facts.

Support, Concern and Respect towards Others

These people believe that other individuals have good qualities within themselves and they make it a habit of acknowledging them one by one as soon as they experience it. This clearly shows their respect towards other individuals.

Another good thing about them is while they seem reticent in showing their emotions or how they perceive others they would help whenever they feel people need them to provide insights which could be helpful in managing problematic situations. These are people who are quick in showing care and compassion to persons whom they feel needs it most. This quality makes them one of the most ideal persons to be with.

Work and Finances

ISFJs may not find it hard to maintain connections whether professional or personal because of their habit of being good at storing details; a very unusual attribute for introverts like them. Even though they are good at maintaining ties, they never go beyond the point of using connections to further their own personal end. They would even dwell on limiting themselves into being semi-close of what used to be a real close relationship before a friend earned a promotion.

These kindhearted people are hardworking and use more effort in order to fulfill goals, promises; and duties and obligations to them are serious topics. Being good listeners, their organizational skills are excellent that is why day-to-day needs are met accordingly. Managing their finances is one of their best points just as their desire to seek lifelong commitments.

Society

Doing things using the tried and tested way is another habit that ISFJ individuals have. They have deep respect for tradition as well as the law. They are unlike other personalities who dwell on ways that are not socially acceptable which could affect relationships and social standing. Tradition, to them, is far more important than using other rules to meet their personal needs.

ISFJs are known to be meticulous, patient and analytical which is a weird combination but makes them effective in many fields. Given the liberty, they may lack skill in embracing novel and radical approaches but their sheer passion and determination can make up for it. They may defend what is existing but not totally blinded towards possibilities of change as long as the new procedures do not contradict their values or principles.

Family
Family is always placed on top priority for the ISFJ personality besides from being effective in the workplace. They believe that members of their families are the most valuable people; thus, providing them with their needs and offering their fervent emotional support. However, they are prone to become overly doting which can transform them into being obsessive in nature.

Negative Traits

Some downsides to being ISFJs may be similar to other types of personalities. Listed below are among the most common ones.

1. ISFJs tend to acquire pent up frustration as they leave some of their thoughts unexpressed. Although they are good at sizing-up people, they may not be very vocal about it that is why anxiety or tension buildup is more likely to happen within their systems.

2. The tendency of neglecting their own needs may come as a result of giving in or catering to the needs of others and this may prove to be daunting for ISFJ individuals at times.

3. Like the ISTJs, they may find it hard to say 'no' which leaves them with loads of work but there are few of them who are capable of refusing whenever they see that their plates are full. This is a good move in order not to be exploited by superiors or other coworkers.

4. If we see the ISTPs as skillful in moving on after ending a relationship, these so-called nurturers would fail on this department. They would even find it hard to shift to another field of endeavor.

5. This type of personality would succumb to understating achievements earned and is not into

advertising them. This may stand in the way of future promotions or recognition from people they work for. This makes them less visible in certain professional circles and may cause them some insecurities. It goes to show that they have to use some tricks for their work to be appreciated so as to be seen and prevent themselves from battling bouts of stress due to conflicts and criticisms.

6. Because they have a habit of trying hard to surpass other people's expectations, there is a tendency of becoming overbearing which may irk or annoy other personality types. Conflicts may arise unless other personality types learn about the good qualities of the ISFJs.

Careers Suitable for the ISFJ Personality

Many people of this type may have been aware that they have landed on the right careers but others remained in a quandary if they are into the right path. The following fields of work may be suitable for the ISFJ personality and may serve as guide for those who are not yet aware of their strong points.

1. *Health Care Department:*
   - Nurse or Licensed Practical Nurse (LPN)
   - Veterinarian
   - Primary Care Physician or Family Physician
   - Pharmacist/Pharmacy Technician

- Dental Hygienist
- Medical Technologist
- Physical Therapist
- Dietician/Nutritionist
- Optician
- Home Health Aid
- Radiological Technician
- Respiratory Therapist
- Medical/Dental Assistant
- Medical Equipment Sales
- Health Care Administrator
- Medical Records Administrator

2. *Technical/Creative Side:*
   - Retail Owner
   - Innkeeper
   - Artist/Musician
   - Interior Decorator
   - Electrician
   - Preferred Customer Sales Representative
   - Merchandise Planner

3. *Real Estate Business:*
   - Agent
   - Broker

4. *Social Service and Education Fields:*
   - Preschool/Elementary Teacher
   - Special Education Teacher

- Librarian/Archivist
- Guidance Counselor
- Educational Administrator
- Social Worker
- Religious Educator
- Speech Pathologist
- Probation Officer
- Curator
- Home Health Social Worker
- Personal or Child Welfare Counselor
- Alcohol and Drug Addiction Counselor
- Genealogist

5. *Business Careers:*
- Customer Service Representative
- Computer Operator
- Bookkeeper
- Credit Counselor
- Personnel Administrator
- Clerical Supervisor or Secretary
- Paralegal
- Home Health Care Sales

This type of personality is compatible with people who are on the same personality group they are in and also with the ISTP, ESRF and ISFJ personalities.

Chapter 4
ISFP - The Artist

The ISFP is made up of 5-10% of the population. People may hardly get to know them because they are used to keeping their thoughts to themselves; meaning—their energy is directed mainly inwards. Independent and deliberate as they are, being at the core of everybody else's attention is one thing they hate most. They make good use of their five senses and are spontaneous human beings. Here are some quick facts about the ISFP personality:

Introversion: Tend to be quiet and reserved when around people they are not well-acquainted with. This person may opt to spend more time with family or friends close to them.

Sensing: Focus is directed not mostly on the future of things but for the time being. It is believed that concrete information is more useful than abstract theories.

Feeling: Personal concerns are seen as more essential than logical or objective information.

Perceiving: This individual is open for new concepts and deciding on an option may take a while because he may look for another alternative or indulge on a wait and see attitude before making things final.

Understanding the ISFP

People who belong to this group sense a deep concern towards other people's needs and are wary of their feelings.

29

However, they are susceptible to deciding based on emotions. As they live at the moment, others may see them as carefree individuals. They are creative and their artistry easily enables them to appreciate beauty. These people are easily to get along with even if they hold back onto some aspects of their lives. Their loyalty, adaptability and caring nature easily endears them to many individuals.

ISFPs may differ from each other; while some of them seem aloof, morose or detached, a part of their population seem to favor liberating themselves from this paradigm. Oftentimes, other people with this type of personality would exhibit both and the abrupt transformation may surprise onlookers who may have known them as otherwise.

On some instances, some of them may use luck or gut feel and may not be afraid to take risks. A good number of males who fall under the ISFP group are competitive in sports most especially in table games and losing may devastate them.

ISFP Learning Styles
ISFPs favor a different approach when it comes to learning and organized education is out of the question for the majority. Many of them have a tendency to drop out even before the end of the secondary level. What they would opt for is something based out of experience and a lot of them excel on this style.

These people are good at using the concrete approach that includes hands-on experience and by asking questions from mentors. Learning environments they favor mostly are those which can provide them with artistic outlets or something that shows a little variety.

On Relationships

This particular type of personality exhibits warmth and friendliness after they are at ease with people they have relationships with. However, they get easily offended by those who appear domineering and unfeeling towards other individuals.

Their affair with nature is one of their best traits; they love animals and the outdoors. They would usually seek jobs that enable them to get in contact with nature.
They keep their relationships private and refuse to reveal them in public. Their trust and loyalty towards their connections, whether it be personal or professional attachments, are traits other personalities find appealing. Most of the time, they would defer revealing secrets if these are found to create possible conflicts between individuals or could contradict a thought presented by some members of the group.

Work and Career
The skills and other abilities that are normally found in this kind of personality is their greatest contribution to society. Their excellence in using tools and skillfulness in solving problems are additions to their positive traits. They would rather dwell on helping others in different types of tasks than see them fumbling due to inexperience.

Strong values emanate naturally from ISFPs but it does not mean they have to push others to accept what they believe in. They are people who know how to step back and give way for others to say what's on their minds and not among those who believe that heavy convincing is key to successful team operations.

Their artistic side makes them the most creative of all personality types. But altogether, they are people who desire to hear compliments from their peers or within the home.

Comparing the ISFPs with other Personality Types

- ISFPs tend to dwell less on the fantasy world compared to the INFS personality. As people may take these two types as similar to each other, the latter are found to lean more towards daydreaming or poetic and philosophical pursuits. On the other hand, ISFPs lean more on their id experiences.

- If the ISFJ individuals are more conventional and use "shoulds and have-to's", ISFPs are masters in internalizing their emotions which come out spontaneously and disappear as fast as it mysteriously came.

- Due to varying feeling judgment expressions people confused them with the ESFJ personality at certain points; the only difference lies in their being aloof and reservation and the latter's ability to expose what they feel.

- ISFJs are good at performing tasks wherein everybody can see them but not quite good at talking about their fears while ESFPs fall on the opposite side.

How ISFPs Fare

The ISFP personality possesses strengths and weaknesses that may surpass the others. Here is a rundown of their plus and minus factors.

Strengths

- It appears that they are strong in their sense of adaptability towards any kind of situation or relationships. This is true because of their wait and see attitude which makes them think first before reacting to any kind of challenge.

- Taking commitments seriously using their laid back personality is a plus factor which is not always found in other types of personalities.

- Listening skills for them is a powerful tool that enhances their ability to establish real friendships and other relations.

- Their easy-going attitude makes it easy for them to accept other people for who they are.

- Another thing that separates them from the rest is their artistic side that results to a no-nonsense creative approach that other individuals may envy.

Weaknesses

33

- Other people belonging to other types may find them unmotivated and difficult to get close with due to their reserved nature although it is only a way for them to weigh things out.

- When a surge of complex situations arise, these people have a tendency to withdraw but sometimes, this trait is helpful and enables them to plan the next move.

- Long term planning which other personalities find beneficial is not a usual trait for ISFPs. They take things as they come.

- They can be their own critics due to their perfectionist nature. The high expectations they place on themselves are factors that lead them to underestimate and at times undervalue their effort and skills.

Careers Appropriate for ISFPs

Their ability to focus on what is imminent makes the ISFPs skilled at careers concerning practical applications and real-world problems. They would choose to indulge a great deal on jobs that provide them with freedom or that which offer them the capacity to act on their own—using the least supervision.

Below are some of the suitable jobs for ISFPs: Artist

- Composer or musician

- Designer

- Nurse

- Psychologist

- Teacher

- Social worker

- Naturalist

- Pediatrician

- Forest ranger

- Veterinarian

- Chef

However, ISFPs are not limited to these jobs alone as some of them may find it challenging to work on other fields they deem as their waterloo. These individuals can be motivated by personalities coming from: ISFP, ESFP, ESTJ or ISTJ.

Chapter 5

INFJ - The Protector

The INFJ is considered as the rarest among personality types and the least found in men besides from being the third least personality type found in women. Statistics show that only 2% out of the general population is composed of this type that includes 2% females and 1% males.

The protector is characterized mainly as quiet but strong personality that prefers original and sensitive approach to life. People who fall under this personality trait never leave a stone unturned until they are done with their tasks.

Their overall characteristic is formed by introversion, intuition, feeling and judging traits. They are well-known individuals who possess individualistic, persevering and owning well-developed sense of values.

Digging Deeply into the INFJ Personality

People under the INFJ personality thrive on their strong sense of uprightness and drive themselves into helping others to realize their goals and other potentials. They help create original solutions to personal challenges as well. Their gift of intuition makes them aware of another person's emotions even before he gets to know it exists.

One could spot an INFJ through their quiet attribute. They care for other people's plight and listen attentively to another person's concerns or ideas. Belonging to a complex type of personality makes it easier for them to deal with complicated situations.

Nonetheless, persons who don the INFJ personality trait are very private individuals who are reluctant in engaging conversations with others whom, they think, might not share the same views, understand or appreciate their own outlook. These people are cautious when it comes to revealing feelings and thoughts. That is why people think they are difficult to know.

Although they have this reserved character, they are genuinely willing to help other people without waiting for recognition and in many instances they act even just by themselves.

Values

Guided by a set of deeply considered personal values, INFJs stay loyal towards what they believe in and will never follow other individuals into dwelling with values that are not found to be authentic. Once they sense another's intentions are not pure or there is no respect towards their set of values, their reaction is to withdraw.

These people may surprise other personalities with the intensity they possess as soon as their values are either questioned or threatened. The calmness in their appearance is the opposite of their real nature. On a lighter note, INFJs are highly motivated due to the targeted values they have and are very much persistent on taking positive action. This drive is essential in their goal of creating a better world.

Hobbies

INFJs are fond of doing things that people consider as branching from the arts. These hobbies include:

- Art Appreciation
- Music (playing or listening)
- Writing
- Cultural Events
- Reading

- Socializing (involving small groups)

Strengths and Weaknesses

Among the strengths of the INFJs is their non-stop exploration for self-growth, development and learning which makes them one of the most adaptive personalities in the Jungian theory. Adding to this list is their dedication to achieving ultimate relationship and ability to move on after one has ended.

Besides their attentive nature, INFJs are skilled at communication most especially in written form. Some of their traits found on the opposite end are the tendency to hide their private affairs. INFJs are not good at managing finances and they even fail at handling daily necessities.

Having high expectations towards themselves and to others can either be a weakness or strength. Their idealistic nature which propels them to picture out a perfect future for them and their families may be a diversion so as not to become discouraged by present day harsh realities.

Relationships

INFJs search for a life that is meaningful. This is the reason for establishing deep connections with other people and helping them in the complexities of life. However, these people are not sold out to the idea of sharing everything in them with everybody except for a selected few. For them, relationships must be real and true, and secrets can only be shared with those they trust the most.

Romantic and Sexual Involvement

It is in their perfectionist trait that makes them idealistic which can be a good quality a lot of people love to see in relationships. These people enjoy displaying their love and in return, they want to see their mates reciprocate the same. At times, their mates feel frustrated because they fear they may not be perfect in the eyes of the INFJs. Nonetheless, the display of depth in the caring department, which is not a common characteristic in other types, is surely an indication of a sincere commitment.

INFJs see sexual intimacy as next to a spiritual experience. When they bond intimately with their partners, they make sure that both heart and mind work all together. There is a need for them to make their partners happy and see intimacy as a tool they can use in providing selfless love.

However, as they gear up to seek perfection in relationships, they always end up jumping from one to another as they have a difficulty in finding long standing romantic ties. INFJs find both the ENFP and ENTP as their natural match. In short, their introverted intuition matches what is innate in people with extroverted intuition.

INFJ as Friends

Friends of the INFJs value the way they treat them because they put effort in investing on the relationship by means of bringing out the best in them. They have friends from different personality types but hate people who are dishonest and may continually avoid being seen with them.

The INFJ personality is quite popular as evidenced by a lot of people drawn towards them. But INFJs are not always aware of the popularity or conscious about being with a flock of friends and acquaintances at certain times because they don't give it much importance.

The INFJ Parents

INFJ parents place more importance on guiding their children into becoming independent, growth-oriented and responsible adults. They give way for their offspring to be heard during family discussions. They teach them how to be self-reliant and good and skilled at making the right decisions.

Also, they can be demanding and expect too much from their children. Whenever their expectations are not met and although they are soft-spoken individuals, they can transform into sharp-tongued individuals. This is also true when they are under stressful situations.

INFJs are serious about their parenting role and are able to make sacrifices for the sake of their young. They believe in prioritizing passing on the values they have to their children. In the end, they will come to realize that conflicting beliefs are not signs of failure but something that speaks of success in rearing children who have learned to adapt their ideals.

INFJs at the Workplace

What INFJ individuals like to land into jobs that may enable them to practice leadership. They would seek something which can make them grow as individuals or progress into another providing them with more independence.

Some may prefer to practice on their own as sole business proprietors in order to have more room for changes which they think can make them advance to another level using their own strategies.

Their most likely jobs would be in the fields of:

- Music
- Design
- Art
- Photography
- Writing (blogs, screenplays, stories, etc)

Other available options are those which can lead them towards spirituality, morality or personal growth; themes that are serious for other types of personalities.

They should avoid are jobs that involve:

- Auditing
- Accounting
- Data Analysis
- Cold-call Sales
- Legal Prosecutor or Defense Attorney
- Corporate Politics

Rank and file INFJ individuals are likely to get annoyed when imposed with hard rules and routine tasks. They value diplomacy and favor a more democratic approach in the workplace. It is where they feel their values or inputs are of great value and when this happens, they find happiness and satisfaction with their jobs. However, once they receive criticisms and unwarranted complaints, their morale would sink to the lowest levels.

The manager INFJs are people who are hesitant in exercising authority over their subordinates as they want to treat them as their equals. They would rather choose to inspire or motivate rather than to whip them hard to make them work well or compensate for their salaries.

The INFJ personality may find the ENFJ, INTP, ENTP and fellow INFJs compatible with their own personality.

Chapter 6

INFP - The Idealist

The INFP or the idealist type ranks 9th most common personalities in the population which means it covers approximately 4%. It is composed of 4% males and 5% females with hobbies ranging poetry, music, creative writing and theater. Other favored pastimes of the Introversion, Intuition, Feeling and Perception type are the visual arts and photography; both of which are also found in INFP individuals.

Traits Innate of the INFPs

The idealist in every INFP individual makes them aware that every worst person or event has something positive to show that is why they search for ways that can make things better.

Their uniqueness may be seen in the following traits:
- They are at high risk of being misunderstood until they find people who have almost the same traits as theirs with whom they can spend time with.

- INFPs are steered by their own standards rather than excitement, logic, or practicality. They are guided by their pure intent and not by punishments and rewards. However, there are INFP individuals who

43

may lead themselves towards isolation once there is no clear understanding of the drives that set them in motion.

- INFPs are able to genuinely communicate with others by using metaphors or parables and creating symbols in order to explain their ideas.

- This personality type's ability in communicating does not end at their native tongue; they are some kind of linguists who are capable of learning various languages.

The Romantic Side of the INFPs

INFP individuals tend to dream about perfect relationships almost all the time. They have this pre-drawn image of their ideal mate or partner whom they would seem to place on a pedestal. They believe that couples can be happier together than living alone and that both can make an effort to make that sought after relationship come true.

INFPs focus their attention not towards too many individuals but only a few. This is a known quality of the Prospecting types who feel that there is no rush in committing themselves into a relationship. This wholehearted approach enables them to explore thoroughly before they settle with whom they feel is most compatible with their own personality.

Therefore, they feel that there is a need for comparison until they arrive at a perfect match. This process can pose as a real challenge as their partners may not capable of keeping up with their set standards.

In times conflicts arise, INFPs can end the relationship quickly and accept the fact that the bond or union was not meant to be. With this, they will then start to look for another individual who owns their ideal qualities. Removing themselves from an unhappy relationship is a trait most natural in this type of individuals as they dislike conflict. Nonetheless, aside from being passionate towards people they care about, respect towards them is preserved.

These are individuals highly susceptible to internalizing ideas and can become highly objective even with statements or facts. They do this because they think that anything presented in front of them may threaten the foundations of their beliefs. This overreaction leads people to consider that there are several points that INFP individuals must work on.

As partners, they are ideal as they stay true to themselves and have the ability to encourage their mates to do the same. They put effort in trying to know their partners better by using physical intimacy and understanding their needs and wants. Being generous in affection, they make sure their mates are satisfied by the pleasure they provide which in turn provide them with the same feeling as well.

Weaknesses of INFPs

As always, there are weaknesses to every personality just as there are strong points. Here are some aspects that show INFP individuals are also human beings who are highly capable of mistakes and errors.

- Respond to baseless accusations: INFPs should focus on enhancing their ability to react to criticism by using calmness

- Focus attention towards a few: They should learn to widen their connections, relationships or activities in order not to feel easily disappointed or dejected whenever things turn out bad

- Tend to neglect day-to-day upkeep: If they are not careful, INFPs stand to lose themselves in their search for goodness out of others or looking out for positive outcomes for their endeavors or activities

- Always preoccupied: They may withdraw into hermit mode which friends and family find it hard to bring them back into normal life

- Have a wrong connotation relationships: They think that perfect relationships happen in a magical way and blind at the fact that it can only be obtained when there is understanding, compromise and effort.

The INFP on Friendships

The number of true friends of the INFP personality is fewer than those belonging to other types but few as they are these friends are to stay on for the rest of their lives.

The many challenges this personality type faces is huge due to several dualities when talking about being sociable as they may be seen in the following situations:

- While INFPs long for the intensity of mutual understanding, they easily get tired when in social situations.

- They have proven themselves as excellent in reading others' feelings or motivations, but oftentimes not willing to provide the same towards themselves

- It appears that the INFPs favor human contact, but not the totality of social contact because they limit potential friends in their effort of preserving their private life, values and inner cores

- These individuals may want to hold on to their mysterious quality even though they have already established friendly relations with other people

- They have greatness in terms of being sensible towards others but this relaxed attitude can only be there for a certain length of time as they would remove themselves from the crowd after which they re-enter their own space

The Parents inside INFP Individuals

Not only INFPs strive to share their own principles and guide other individuals in their quest for learning and growth; they are also keen on finding greater opportunities in parenthood. It is in their parenting roles that they give their best besides being good at other personalities.

Here are some of their parenting characteristics:

- People belonging to the INFP personality type are good at providing their children the freedom they need to learn, explore and grow. In line with this aim they keeping an open mind and allow them to catch up with their own thoughts and ambitions.

- They are highly supportive of their children's own endeavors and unceasing in inspiring and motivating them in every step of the way. They make use of speaking in their children's language so that they will both understand each other.

- The protection they provide their offspring reaches great lengths as while they shield them from the harshness the outside world offers, they also protect them from their own anxiety or anger.

- They stand as quality role models by educating them about moral lessons and demonstrating what is right.

- Their ability to instill goodness in their children is possible when partnered with a stronger personality who is more skilled at administrative tasks.

Careers for the INFP

The INFPs are at liberty in choosing people they get to work with because of the many things they are capable of and being good at doing them. They feel they are required to win people's attention.

Careers that they would possibly be into or take interest in are:

- Massage therapy
- Physical rehabilitation
- Counseling
- Social work
- Psychology
- Academic Jobs

After all, these are people who take preference in using their own personal touch, working with clients face-to-face and making sure that their effort would create impact on another individual's life.

Chapter 7

INTJ - The Scientist

Being labeled as independent, analytical, original and determined is no joke and these qualities make up most of the INTJ personality. They are known to be the most practical and having the most amount of self-confidence of all personality types.

INTJ people, who comprise 1% of the population have Introverted, Intuitive, Thinking and Judging as their main descriptors. They love to dwell on logical ideas and are easily drawn towards scientific research or study due to their fondness for accuracy and precise thinking.

Other traits of the INTJ are:

- Capable of turning theories into concrete action plans
- Value knowledge, structure and keen on competence
- Ambitious and derive meaning out of their visions
- Think of long-range plans
- Have high standards when it comes to performance
- Natural-born leaders

The Real INTJs

Observers see the INTJs have an aura of being definite and usually mistaken as arrogant.

This may be attributed to their knowledge in special systems that INTJs have already learned at a young age. Ask an INTJ personality about things pertaining to their several areas of expertise and they will readily tell you about it or teach you on what you require them to do. They may remain honest by telling people what they are not capable of doing.

Their perfectionism trait enables them to produce an independent mind that is free from convention, authority constraints or sentiments. The system builder trait in them shows their reliability and creative imagination. Due to these qualities, they would tend to be rigid on those found slacking on performing duties and responsibilities and may even reprimand them for being so.

INTJs have the habit of implementing decisions without prior consultation from their coworkers or supervisors. They easily take it on themselves to seize opportunities which others may not have seen as there in the first place. Simply put, this is how observant this personality type is.

At Work
The Keirsey Temperament has its own version of the INTJ wherein individuals of this type are referred to as the mastermind. Masterminds like the INTJ individuals are referred to as excellent in contingency planning and this makes them stand out from the rest. INTJ individuals are not usually seen outside factories, offices, schools or laboratories. These are people who are clearly fond of creating alternative routes to use in cases where plan A did not work.

Although they are regarded by many as leaders, they will wait until the person in command fails to do what is needed before they step in and take charge or lead the rest. Upon assuming leadership, they would only put to use ideas which make sense in order to reach maximum work efficiency.

They would rather work for long periods and dedicate their time in pursuing their goals than staying idle. Problem solving is what they find stimulating as they respond to fix tangled tasks by sorting them thoroughly. For them, to move forward is more important than to dwell on past mistakes.

Once the INTJ practices tolerance and uses some effort to effectively translate their thoughts to others he will have the opportunity of leading a prosperous and rewarding life.

Personal Relationships

INTJs care deeply for a selected few and eager to spend time and effort on relationships. However, their self-confidence and knowledge can challenge them in their interpersonal relations. This may come as a result of not being able to grasp the rituals of society. They may, as an example, tend to lose patience and lack understanding on small talk or flirtation, which are quite essential in relationships.

Because they are very private individuals, they can be unemotional towards their partners; that is why they would appear to be hard to read or understand. They would demand that things presented to them are those that make sense. Therefore, they expect reasonability and sincerity in everything they feel, hear or see.

On the sexual part of relationships, these individuals would find ways to perfect intimacy. Creativity and sheer sensitivity towards their partners may shine on this aspect but on the negative side of it, some of them might enjoy the thought of performing sex than doing it physically. When this happens, everything becomes theoretical rather than being able to show affection and love.

Maybe, the best attributes they have in the relationship department are their ability to work on a relationship and being intuitive. Even though they are regarded as Thinkers, they do not fully possess natural empathy like what Feelers have.

This lack brings them to use their intuitive function which is a good tool to use to extract possible meanings out of the tone, voice or facial expression. What they can do to counter this is to hone this ability using more consistent effort so as to understand those they care deeply about.

Parenthood

People who belong to the INTJ personality carefully research and prepare strategies as far as parenthood is concerned. Just like the way they deal with a lot of things, they are very thorough individuals. They will stand prepared by reading resources on child rearing, digest all information they have obtained and form conclusions. Once they have drafted their own plans, they are bent on carrying them out.

The only trouble is their habitual sternness that may show when they use discipline of their children. They are people who may not be moved by simple whining. What they expect their offspring to be is what they exhibit themselves. So, there would be willingness to critical thinking, autonomy, and perseverance. Most of all, the children are expected to have achievements.

INTJs may not be aware of it but the more time they spend at work could be a huge challenge their children have to face. Future tells us that what we may have done can lead us to regret. The lack of bonding may lead them to want to regain the time lost while their children were still young. Years passed cannot be brought back again so there would be remorse.

Children with this type of personality as parents would grow to become individuals who earned the traits of their parents. He will grow up trusting that their parents are there to take care of their basic needs and know why it is essential to conform to how they are guided.

These are children who would become self-sufficient adults in the future who know how to value the words "efficiency and hard work". This will be the most important legacy that INTJ parents will leave behind.

Weaknesses Found in INTJs

- Their precision and accuracy causes the INTJs inflexibility as they may disregard ideas posed by others who they thought of not owning the ideas like their own.

- They easily feel pressured if their solutions and plans fall short of their normal standards. This causes them to dwell on ideas that may be unproductive or meaningless.

- INTJs may become disagreeable or argumentative individuals when under stress which leads them to experience difficulty in dealing with social interaction.

- Once they lose trust in their own abilities, they would become obsessed with ideas like being inept, weak or afraid that others may find out of their mistakes.

- They spend more time dwelling with their own thoughts that may cause them not to have interest in other people's ideas or emotions.

- They are oftentimes misunderstood because of their ability to pass quick judgments; thus, they are seen as elitist or arrogant. They always think that they are right in a lot of things.

Careers for the INTJs

Careers typical of INTJ individuals are in the fields of Science and Engineering but not really limited to such. They can be well-ensconced in the academe, legal profession or something in line with business. However, they can always go and seek other careers that they find challenging.

Below is a list of possible career matches for the INTJ:

- Scientist
- Mathematician
- Biomedical Researcher
- Psychologist
- Neurologist
- Computer Programmer
- Environmental Planner
- Curriculum Designer
- Administrator
- Management Consultant
- Financial Planner
- Strategic Planner
- New Business Developer
- Economist
- Civil Engineer
- Designer
- Inventor
- Editor
- Art Director
- Info-Graphics Designer
- Intellectual Properties Attorney
- Judge

This type of personality is highly compatible with those who belong to the ENTJ, INFP, ENFP or fellow INTJ personalities.

Chapter 8

INTP - The Thinker

INTPs are quite rare, covering a meager 3% of the population. They take pride on their inventive and creative skills, the unique perspective they have and dynamic intellect. Commonly known as the architect, philosopher or the dreamy professor, INTPs lean towards discoveries and have been known to have so many contributions throughout history of science.

These are people who try their best to seek clarity and unrelenting logic in almost everything around them. People refer to them as the absent-minded professors; logical enough when asked but display no interest in either leading or following a certain leader.

Here are other quick facts that could give away the INTPs:

- Approach problems with enthusiasm but with skepticism
- Ignore existing rules but define own approach towards their resolution
- Critical analysts
- Extremely bright individuals
- Love novel ideas and desire to discuss new concepts with others
- Hate routine work
- Prefer establishing complex solutions based on theories and leave them to be implemented by other people

- Tolerant and adaptive towards people and environment

What Characterizes the INTP

The creative thinker in all INTPs comes out whenever they hear original and logical theories or ideas. They are exceptionally quick in understanding these theories even with their quiet and reserved attitudes. Their competence may have sprung from their preference to value knowledge and internal focus.

The Introverted INTPs are normally shy when surrounded by new people. However, they are quite confident and gregarious when with those they have known before. This type of personality thinks that facts or ideas should be presented correctly as they themselves express ideas which they believe are true.

They can do away with traditional goals like security and popularity due to their complex characters which lean towards being restless and temperamental. Their ingenious and unconventional mind patterns enable them to evaluate ideas in a lot of ways that brings forth many options to create or solve any kind of problem. This is one of the reasons why the INTPs are what people call the Scientists.

They have a tendency to share ideas even though they are not yet fully developed. This shows them using other people as sounding boards for their plans and theories to extract comments, reactions or suggestions rather than establishing conversation.

Although at times they are found to be in a dreamy mode because their brains are endlessly processing facts, this mood may change when unfamiliar faces are around; even a friendly joke may turn the atmosphere into a combative one as a result of difference of opinions.

As a rule INTPs move from one topic or another before the first one gets to be understood by their audiences and these usually complex topics are never laid out in a simple manner.

Once they find an atmosphere where their creativity and potential can be put across, the INTP knows no bounds when it comes to time and energy as they will gladly expend on developing insightful and impartial solutions. But people have to take note that these individuals are not so much into worrying about their practical activities or lifestyles.

Where strengths of the INTPs lie:

- **Analytical and Abstract Thinking** - They see the humanity as a big and complex machinery with a belief that all parts are connected. INTPs stand out where analyzing these links are concerned and see how apparently unrelated factors connect in ways that baffle other personality types.

- **Imagination and Originality** - Their ideas may look counter-intuitive at first and which to others would seem as flash in the pan. These ideas, however, may prove to be remarkable innovations in their own right.

- **Open-Mindedness** - INTPs are extremely receptive to other people's theories if they're supported by facts or logic. They are fairly liberal and believe that other's opinions also matter.

- **Enthusiasm** - Whenever a new idea captures their interest, they take it enthusiastically. Even with their reserved attitude, they find time in discussing it. People just have to be reminded not to get affected by the way they carry themselves as even though they are already excited to hear about a new development, they might still sport a morose facial expression or any other gesture that does not seem to fit the word eagerness.

- **Objectivity** – INTPs see themselves as channels for truths that surround them and take pride of exercising the role of a theoretical mediator.

- **Honesty and Simplicity** - INTPs are not fond of intentionally going around hurting people's feelings. To them, the truth is an essential factor and that it has to be appreciated and reciprocated by people.

Weaknesses of INTPs

- **INTPs do not value decisions based on personal subjectivity**: They feel that these offer no relevance in decision-making. This trait shows that they are unable to decipher other people's feelings; a reason which disables them to meet emotional needs of their peers or other relations.

- **Not likely to understand emotional grievances at all**: Friends will never find them lending emotional support. Instead, they would present suggestions to resolve underlying issues to the dismay of people who expect to get something concrete out of the complaints.

- **Social rebellion and self-aggrandizement comes in the way of their creativity**: Their Feeling trait is the least developed that is why INTPs find it hard to provide warmth or support which are vital ingredients in relationships. They may be observed to be sarcastic or found excessively critical of others.

- **Weak in maintenance-type jobs**: Tasks such as personality management or to the least—paying bills. This display of absent-mindedness shows their under-developed sensing side.

- **Not sold to the idea of explaining further**: There are many ways for other people to understand what INTPs are trying to point out but these people are not bent on explaining to make way for easy comprehension. This goes the same with customizing a truth in order for others to know its essence.

- **Prone to jump to another project or tasks**: Just when they have figured out how a task works or believe that it will work out fine, INTPs would go to another project leaving the project to other people or leave it alone to stand alone.

- **Effects of their withdrawn Personality**: Their shyness is seen during large gatherings which make even their close friends struggle in order to get through their heart and mind.

- **Neglecting Rules and Guidelines** - Social struggles may result from INTP individuals' desire to find a way around set rules of conduct or other guidelines meant for the society to follow. While this is a plus factor for creativity, at times, the need to constantly reinvent their own guidelines may affect people or situations.

- **Delaying output**: They seek for progress or improvement on their work but they would always think that their current work is only second best to what they can actually do. They would carry out several revisions to perfect their craft but unable to arrive at the best outcome delays actual output.

- **Unaware of other's emotional needs:** They may not know it at times but they are not aware that their colleagues, friends, family members or partners are already experiencing some kind of emotional problems. They are ignorant to see and feel the need of other people.

INTPs on Relationships

INTPs have a combination of traits that other people note as interesting. Even though they are full of ideas, they are unable to explore fully their romantic side. But on the other end, the INTPs would take their relationships very seriously and believe the importance of being involved with someone. These surprisingly loyal individuals also have the notion that establishing mutual understanding and expressing what's on their minds help to lessen future misunderstandings and conflict.

They have simple needs which make them overlook that there are some things that are needed to boost relationships like gifts, surprises and dates that involve a little spending. These material things are what friends, family or special people in their life are looking forward to receive.
Friendships may be another aspect that INTPs have to enhance as sincere friendships can go a long way. However, what they look for in friends is intellectual depth so it is not that easy to be friends with them unless there are common goals, interests or thoughts.

Communicating with people is always reserved for meaningful topics or with people they already know can provide them with the same level of intelligence or worth.

INTPs are intensely devoted towards their children; not in the traditional way, though. They are committed to encouraging them to act and think independently, seek for more knowledge and defend their opinions. By allowing their offspring to explore the things around them, they stand by them to overlook minor problems that would surface along the way.

What INTPs need most is a partner more capable of supporting and reminding them what they have missed performing not only inside the home but with work as well. If they are hardworking and creative individuals, they are also excellent at developing fair interpretations of their colleagues' motivations although they may over-think and become suspicious of them.

They are very tolerant and flexible when managing other subordinates as they are open to suggestions. However they have standards that are high which they expect their subordinates to grasp immediately. Partnering with somebody who knows how to filter the thoughts of the INTP can direct the working team into a more successful bid at being productive.

Careers and Compatibility

Mainly, INTPs' love for explorations makes them ideal to work as mathematicians, career scientists or systems analysts. They may also look forward to employing in fields that require exemplary skills in physics. These are individuals who think that being good enough is never enough because they know that they can do more.

This type of personality is perfect when paired with their fellow INTPs and ENTP, INFJ or ENFJ personalities.

Chapter 9
ESTP - The Doer

The ESTPs are friendly, action-oriented and highly adaptive individuals who aim at getting the fastest results. Their lifestyle is fast-paced and people who have this type of personality like to live at the moment. They have extreme loyalty towards their peers and are not particularly fond of listening to long explanations.

These people are not really mindful when it comes to rules and laws. They will try their best to bend them if ever they come in the way when they are trying to get things done.

The ESTP personality makes up 4% of the general population which includes 6% males and 35 females. They would like to indulge in sports or any athletic pursuit; mainly team sports or other risky activities.

ESTP Characteristics

ESTPs are confident and fun to be with. People get easily drawn towards them due to their wit and charm, spontaneous and clever traits and most of all—their ability to deal with emergency situations. These big kids (as other people refer to them), are funny but capable of controlling their temperament. They enjoy taking risks and are excellent at improvisations.

Other traits that best describe these individuals are:

- Straightforward
- Love fine things

- Know how to shower their loved ones with gifts
- Decides based on facts and logic
- Highly perceptive
- Unfazed by conflict
- Spends quality time with their children
- Good storytellers
- Strongly stick to their own beliefs
- Natural-born entrepreneurs
- Highly innovative
- Good at motivating others
- Quick at decision-making
- Sensual individuals

ESTPs are mainly characterized by Extroversion, Sensing, Thinking and Perceiving traits which make them generally outgoing extroverts and enjoy time with huge crowds and acquaintances.

Other manifestations of the ESTPs are as follows:

- They are more interested in the "now" than looking at the future of things.

- With their primary modes focused internally, they absorb things through their five senses (literally).

- On the other hand, they deal with many aspects using the logical and rational way which shows they have a secondary mode that is focused internally.

- ESTPs are people who approach things in the logical manner and takes objectivity as more essential than personal feelings.

- They are also known for their open-minded habits that makes them shy away from excessive planning.

- As experts are heard saying, nobody is more socially sophisticated than ESTPs.

- They are suave and so polished that they can sell any idea to anybody.

- They know how to manipulate people in a subtle manner.

- Their ability to wear different hats stirs everyone and that makes them very exciting individuals to be with.

Notable Weaknesses of ESTPs

Insensitive: ESTPs are noted for not being sensitive towards others' feelings and would tend to hurt them using insensitive language. But of course, they don't mean to, and unfortunately, they are not so choosy with words.

Hate routines: Although they belong to the intelligent lot, they think that school is such a grueling chore that they want to get past it right away. Some of them may drop out from school due to the routine learning styles of particular educational establishments.

High Risk-Takers: People with this trait are good at financial management but then, they take high risks at times. They can be risk-takers when it comes to gambling which is a negative trait.

Hate Long-Term Plans: They are not good at planning for long-range because they easily get bored and want to see the outcome of their work. This is also true with relationships; they may even leave as soon as they get bored!

Generous: But while this is so, they feel the need of showering their loved ones with material things which can be both regarded as strength and weakness.

Bossy and Fails at Follow-throughs: These individuals tend to be bossy around the workplace and may get somewhat unscrupulous in getting things done. They are good and highly motivated to start on projects but eventually, following through tasks is not on their menu.

On Relationships
Their enthusiasm towards other things is carried on to their personal relationships which they want to approach on a day-to-day basis. This means no fast and early commitments. Fun and excitement is always around in all corners of their homes.

As lovers, ESTPs are quite generous, sensual and earthly human beings. No partner can disregard the vast display of affection these individuals can offer. However, some partners are not at all good at this environment because they would value commitment more than anything in the world which to them is a sign of curtailing their freedom.

As soon as this problem develops into a conflict, the ESTP personality will find a way out and may be seen jumping from one relationship to another just because they see commitment as uncomfortable.

Parenting Role

- As parents, ESTPs are fond of playing with their children; they are kids in their own right. This makes it easier to communicate with their young. Not all children listen to their parents; so, the deviant ones may take interest in what their parents may want to impart. They are known to be very skilled at using language that can easily penetrate their kids.

- Kids look at ESTP parents more than their friend and not somebody who like to instill discipline on them. Children may find their voices heard inside their homes and that makes teaching (for the parent) and learning the ropes of life (for the children) more enjoyable. This shows that both may benefit from this style of parenting.

But on top of this is the difficulty ESTP parents will encounter when issuing punishment or discipline among his brood. Because of their easy-going attitude, they are more likely to pass on the discipline aspect to their partners. More often than not, this poses as a conflict between couples but many have found their way into developing strategies to counter this problem.

Friendships

One of the strongest characteristics of the ESTP personality is their ability of being good at people. Being observant, they are good at adapting to other types of personalities. However, they are not at all compatible with those who belong to the Intuitive Thinking type as theoretical and abstract are the opposites of action which the "Doer" ESTP manifests.

The talkative ESTPs form lifelong friendships and the loyalty and love for nature are among the aspects people look for in friendships. But somehow, there are some individuals who belong to this personality group who are otherwise.

This may come as a result of boredom like when a friend talks about things other than what the ESTP finds interesting. Soon enough, the ESTP individual may leave the friendship and move on to another set of friends who share topics or interests they so desire.

The playful and overly active ESTPs are the life of the party wherein their love for humor plays a big role. First, they will assess their audience, then, strike on a conversation that is good enough for everybody to jump in. The athlete in them also makes them easy to tag along with when outdoors. Their love of adventure and use of their skills keep them alive and make them the toast of the open-air playground.

ESTP Personality Best Career Options

ESTPs may opt for jobs that would require them working alongside other people. Without the monotony and routine, they would most likely make good at the following careers:

- Entrepreneur

- Sales agent
- Computer Support Technician
- Marketer
- Police Officer
- Detective
- Paramedic

These fast-paced jobs are ideal for ESTPs because of their different personality characteristics which enable them to suit many fields. They would work perfectly great in positions that require fast-thinking or quick responses.

It's good to know that the ESTP personality is good when together with fellow ESTPs, ISTPs, ESFJs and ISFJs.

Chapter 10
ESTJ - The Guardian

People with the ESTJ personality are rational and logical beings and like the ESTPs, their secondary focus is internal. Their eyes are always there to scan their environment to ensure that everything works systematically and smoothly.

These are people who have a clearly stipulated set of rules and beliefs and honor traditions and other regulations set by the society they live in. While they follow these rules, they expect other individuals to value them.

ESTJ is a personality trait that ranks fifth among the common types (9% of the population), 11% of them males and 6% females. They dwell on more tamed hobbies like gardening, community service and volunteering while some may delve on repairing or building their homes. They also engage in and watch sporting events.

To the experts, they are referred to as the problem solvers; skilled at using and adapting past experiences to answer the call. They are keen on rules or guidelines and ensure that these are carried out to the dot unless people under their supervision are willing to face consequences. ESTJs are individuals who progress from the ranks to land on top of any type of organization.

Traits Natural to ESTJs

Here are traits that would give away ESTJs:

- *Born leaders*: ESTJs are the usual persons-in-charge because of their leadership qualities, confidence and aggressiveness. They are good at evaluating performance, capacity, and compliance just as they look at level of respect for set procedures and schedules.

- *Skilled at plans and systems*: Their skills in devising action plans and systems and their ability to perceive which steps to take makes it easy for them to complete tasks effectively on time.

- *Honest and direct*: ESTJ individuals are honest at their pronouncements and clearly emphasize what they mean. What people see on their faces and whatever comes out of their mouths is the type of people they are.

- *Model Citizens*: These people take commitments seriously and make sure that they tread on the right path as far as social mores are concerned. They use more effort in instilling honesty, dignity and dedication towards a cause or purpose.

- *Fun-loving*: Most of the time, they tend to enjoy activities that involve family, community or people at the workplace. They are also good at bringing people together and may enjoy performing the roles of community organizers.

- *Value-oriented*: They are conscientious, realistic and dependable citizens and workers who take pride in doing things the practical way and being considerate towards others.

- *Takes effort in doing a lot of things*: They see to it that they use the right amount of effort in finding out the relevance of their goals and incorporating them in their search for security and clarity.

- *Generous with Time and Energy*: ESTJs are not stingy when it comes to taking charge of things like service clubs or associations; community organizations or the workforce.

- *Hardworking Individuals*: They were born to be industrious and perform their duties under less or no supervision at all; qualities that came as results of having grown from being model students in school who believe that following instructions is vital to being responsible individuals.

- *Believe in the rule of law and authority*: Many US leaders belong to this trait and they are people who believe that there is nothing more important in society than the belief in the rule of law and authority. They aim to lead by example while rejecting laziness and cheating.

- *Stick heavily on their principles*: Being aware that the environment is capable of change, they make sure that they stick to what they firmly believe in and resist what is not acceptable.

- *Recognize strengths and weaknesses*: They understand that each individual is different and so are their strengths and weaknesses. By this, they would help in leading them towards the right direction wherein everybody works in the same manner as everyone else.

Weak Points Seen in ESTJs

- *Critical and Demanding*: ESTJs can be very critical of others and demanding at times. Due to their strong beliefs, they may voice out what they feel in times when they see somebody is not meeting their expectations. They will not hesitate to give dishonest, lazy or incompetent individuals some kind of fixing.

- *Inflexible*: They are not likely to consider the relevance of goals outside their own scope of understanding. Their inflexibility on this aspect lies on their belief that what they see as values are essential in making society work.

- *Too Detail-Oriented*: People with the ESTJ traits have to be reminded of being overly paying attention to details. Since they tend to put more weight on their beliefs, they neglect that there is a feeling side in other individuals' systems. They might overlook fulfilling other people's need for intimacy that, in long run, would result in hurt feelings.

- *Resort to Isolation*: When under stress, ESTJs have a hard time dealing with the situation. They would tend to isolate themselves from others and feel they are efforts are either undervalued or taken for granted. Although they are known to be vocal individuals, they might find it difficult in communicating with others in situations such as this.

Relationships the ESTJ Way

These hardworking individuals approach relationships and establish human relations also in a traditional way. They have a large circle of friends and many are to stay close with them over several years. They are easy to talk with and quite approachable even at times they seem formal in the way they carry themselves.

ESTJs are fond of social gatherings that they reserve time to attend them as much as their schedules allow them to. They are fond of:
- Class Reunions
- Weddings
- Club Dances

- Awards Banquets
- Holiday Parties

Parenthood and marriage are aspects they hold sacred and make good at. They want things to be in place but provide some space for their partners and children alike to voice out what they feel.

However, their disciplinarian measure would show in their parenting skills as they expect positive outcome out of rearing their offspring. Just like their attitudes when at work, ESTJs take on a managerial role when at home.
Goals are set for everyone to follow and organizing tasks to accomplish within the day or a particular week of the month are written so that productivity even inside the home is observed.

In this case, the children will have to act out as subordinates. This system provides a good result later on in life when they children grow up to be adults. They would find that the systems they have learned at home may provide them with a sense of responsibility which could make them successful individuals.

Careers for the ESTJ Personality

Career paths for ESTJs are just like their traits; clear and straightforward. Though there are other directions for them to go, this personality type always end up where there is a chance to exercise their affinity for structure, organization and follow-through.

ESTJs share a deep respect where tradition, security and stability are concerned; qualities that are vital to progress which can only be obtained through practicing responsibility and dependability. Their loyalty enables them to stay with a single employer longer than other personality types. Their respect for established institutions leads them to work in respectable organizations as well.

Here are careers where ESTJs are bound to work in and perfect for their type of personality:

- Military leader
- Police Officer or Detective
- Auditor
- Financial Officer
- Business Administrator
- Office Manager
- Judge
- Teacher
- Sales Representative

People with ESTJ personality may rise to every occasion to meet obligations using consistent measures which can make them candidates for advancement in any field of endeavor. The ESTJ personality is quite compatible with people who belong to ISTJ, ESFP, ISFP and individuals within their own group.

Chapter 11
ESFP - The Performer

The ESFP personality may be the most spontaneous of all personality types. They are individuals who easily get excited and want other people to feel the same way as they do in a particular time. They make up 9% of the population; 10% of which are women and 7% men.

The ESFP ranks third among the common types and seventh in ranking in most common personality type for men. Among the hobbies they are most likely to engage in are:

- Socializing
- Team sports
- Projects
- Cooking
- Games
- Dance
- Entertaining

Characteristics of the ESFPs

The ESFPs are considered as the friendliest among all types of personalities. They are very easy to deal with and hang around at any time of the day. Their warmth and festivity radiate from within and they exhibit these traits in any kind of situation. These and more characteristics are products of their Extroverted, Sensing, Feeling and Perceiving main traits as exemplified by the Jungian theory.

79

What makes them tick with other people is their love for simple pleasures. They can laugh at anything and their infectious humor makes them the life of the party or any kind of social gathering. Their irrepressible lifestyle attracts a lot of people. They are not used to holding back and may say things that immediately come into their minds and this makes up for their being spontaneous individuals.

Another trait of note is their ability to avoid dwelling on unpleasant events; if bad situations can no longer be converted into fun they would simply drop the topic and move on further to another which is completely different from the stressful one.

ESFPs are born entertainers who love to take center stage and would love to put up a show in front of their friends, family or acquaintances. The way they talk is very appealing to people who are not used to talking for lengths. The attention they get is always at a maximum level as they never run out of catchy topics to use for their storytelling time.

Talking is not just everything for ESFPs as they are:
- Tops in grooming: They are always neat and appropriate
- Fond of well-appointed homes: Their homes speak of their personality
- Fans of great outfits: Able to use conventional outfits but attuned to the latest fashion

Other traits manifested by people with the ESFP personality:
- They are sensitive to other people's feelings. They are quick to note other people's reactions.

80

- ESFPs are able to take the first step in helping someone solve a challenging problem. They are good at assessing the type or magnitude of the problem and always ready to offer emotional support and sensible advice if asked.

- Tend to avoid conflict rather than addressing it head-on. If the conflict involves them, they would shy away or find a diversion.

- They love drama and a little passion but would stop once they see they are being criticized for what they are doing.

- Traditions and expectations are secondary aspects for ESFPs and normally, they never think of these at all.

Strengths of ESFPs

- They love to experiment on new styles alongside with finding new possibilities to stand out from the crowd.

- Their creativity is among their best attribute as it does not limit the aspect on their outfits; they are very articulate and know how to use words that can excite even the dullest conversation.

- They are not into musing on thoughts. They are strong on the practical side wherein they would rather experience a situation than deal with all the what-ifs of the world.

- This group of people own skills that manifest happiness and satisfaction. Witty in every sense of the world, ESFPs are pleasurable people to be with.

- They notice even the minutest detail on people's feelings that is why they earn more trust because of their ability to display empathy towards others.

Weaknesses of the ESFPs

- *Sensitive*: This lot may be seen as sensitive and prone to criticisms just like anyone else. Once they experience negative effects or reactions from people, they may tend to go to a small corner and react badly.

- *Avoiding Conflict*: ESFP individuals will try to avoid conflicts and at times, they would just ignore them. They would go out of their way to move on to a more interesting activity rather than stay behind and get caught in a trap.

- *Get Bored Easily*: ESFPs may create a scenario that could excite their lives just because they get bored easily. They could turn to self-indulgence or risky behaviors when in situations that involve long time waiting.

- Lack of Focus: Long-term plans need more focus and attention which ESFP individuals lack. They would rather read books on psychology than burn their seats relishing academic materials.

There is a need to challenge ESFPs to keep themselves on track for long-term planning and goals. Having a partner who can take this risk or able to curb the negative aspects they have can make ESFPs one of the best personalities ever known by experts.
They have to be reminded that:

1. Refraining from focusing on immediate pleasures can make them take care of their duties and responsibilities; these can, in turn, create a way to make them afford the pleasures they so desired.

2. They have to learn complex analysis and have more patience doing repetitive tasks so as to overcome boredom while at work.

3. Being self-reliant is a better tool in achieving goals than relying on opportunity, luck or asking help from friends.

4. Being poor planners creates irresponsible individuals who may spend more than they can afford.

On ESFP Relationships

These fun-loving and exciting people may not be building relationships for future purposes but only for the time being. Bubbly as they are, their character attracts more pairs of eyes than others can imagine. They would enjoy somebody else's company and savor what life can offer at the moment.

Romantic Side
ESFPs are not in a rush so nothing gets serious until a certain point of time. When enjoyment burns out after a period of time and when this happens, it's time for the ESFP personality to re-evaluate things and learn ways to patch up the relationship. But if the strategy itself is not able to repair the damage, then, calling things off is not a hard thing to do.

If ever an affair lasts longer than previously expected, definitely, it would be a lasting and meaningful one. The ESFPs as lifetime partners offers many positive results and among them is marital satisfaction. It is a known fact that they rank the second highest in marital satisfaction. Nonetheless, they are seen as belonging to the lowest income bracket.

The Parents in every ESFPs
ESFPs are known to be relaxed when it comes to parenting roles. Children would be delighted to have them in their homes because they can experience sheer pleasure when playing with them. They know how to devise ways to make games more exciting which, to other personalities, is somewhat a difficulty.

ESFP parents also know how to impose rules but they have a different approach to disciplining their young. Just because they have made some mistakes in the past, they will do their best in preventing their kids to repeating the same errors. They flood their offspring with emotional support and warmth to fill the gap in between rules.

At Work

ESFPs may find careers that involve achieving fast and concrete results enjoyable more than anything else. This enjoyment may be doubled when people start appreciating their efforts. Working in groups in action-oriented environments is also among their strong points as it provides them with variety and independence.

A flexible and spontaneous working style is another aspect where ESFPs are most interested in. This is in line with their fast decision making skill which puts their subjectivity towards values to work.

Possible Careers for the ESFP

Careers most likely populated by ESFPs are those which fall on being on center stage, requiring other forms of artistry or directly dealing with people like the following:

- Artists
  - o Performers
  - o Actors
- Fashion Designers
- Photographers
- Interior Decorators
- Social Work
- Counselors
- Medical
  - o Child Care

- o Nursing
- Human Resources
  - o Sales Representatives

Compatible personality types for the ESFPs are the ISFPs, ESTJs, ISTJs and fellow ESFs.

Chapter 12
ESFJ - The Caregiver

One of the most common types of personality traits is the ESFJ. People who fall under this group of traits are popular personalities in the community. The ESFJs comprises 12% of the population and are commonly seen as the cheerleaders, team leaders or quarterbacks who usually propel teams towards fame and victory.

These are people who make sure that everything works out fine for the good of the group and see to it that everyone else gets satisfaction and happiness. They stay up-to-date with the goings on of the society, able to maintain or enhance their social standing, and overly concerned of their physical appearance.

These selfless individuals base their morals on set laws and traditions, uphold authority, and understand the meaning of people coming from different backgrounds or ethnicity. What they are more famous of is their love for service which they find very meaningful. The appreciation they gain from it makes them do more.

How to Spot ESFJs

A person can be spotted immediately from a crowd due to a particular type of characteristic. Here are traits that would easily give away the ESFJs:

- *They chat and laugh with everyone*: These are people who can talk with almost anybody due to their wide array of topics and happy experiences to share.

- *Devoted individuals*: Their devotion does not end where the party ends as they can do some fixing where tension is concerned. In short, they will never leave the room unless the smell of good vibes flows around.

- *Fast to adapt*: They are able to adapt to any type of situation like when talking to a person with a different personality trait, ESFJs can change the way they speak or move to please the ones they are facing at a particular moment.

The ESFJ personality is typically conscious regarding gender roles and is more comfortable performing roles that suit their own gender. Male ESFJs are quite masculine and the females are very feminine.

ESFJs who were brought up and surrounded by strong value systems and centered on goodness are the kindest and most generous. Those who grew up in another kind of environment may own twisted ethics and have the tendency to be manipulative or self-centered.

Relationships

ESFJs respect hierarchy and do the best they can to position themselves with people in authority whether at home or at the workplace. They believe that this will allow them to maintain a stable, clear and organized relationship for everyone. ESFJs are loyal and devoted as partners, parents; friends or coworkers.

They are individuals who enjoy hearing about friends' relationships, achievements and activities. Every little detail is always remembered by these warm beings which endear them towards their friends and other relations. The level of energy and well-developed social intelligence earns them hordes of acquaintances and friends.

Parenting: The ESFJ Way

As parents, the ESFJ personality has a huge opportunity to display warmth, dedication and affection in ways that provide positive impact. Sensitive but firm, ESFJ parents are capable of establishing rules and set authority without entirely appearing as overbearing. They use compassion and add a dash of support to smoothen occasional miscommunication or differences in opinion.

Owning children seems to be the culmination of every ESFJ. As children reach adolescence wherein they start pushing away from their parents, ESFJs try their best to manage the transition. They may try to prolong dependency as long as they can handle it. They have the notion that, in doing so, their children will be well-prepared to face the realities of life and this is one accomplishment parents can be proud of.

Another thing to note in ESFJ parents is their skill at administering authority. While they are affectionate of their offspring, they are capable of asserting their traditional views and once it is laid in front of the children, the declaration of authority is final.

The ESFPs as Friends

Nothing could be more hurtful to the ESFJ personality type than knowing a trusted colleague or friend is critical or opposed to their habits and beliefs except when having been told openly or directly. This hurt can be aggravated at times because the ESFJs are people who tend to believe that their friends can do them no wrong as they can defend their friends no matter what the circumstances they are into.

They are quite receptive to their wide circle of friends and receptive towards their perspectives. They may use their own sensitivity to be in tune with what drives and motivates their friends. What drives them is creating a situation that can make them inspire others and encouraging other people fuels their souls as well.

The ESFJ Romantic Side

To ESFJs, romantic relationships are very significant. They are not into the casual fling thing. What they want is to have their partners beside them with whom they would ask for unwavering support. Marriage and children are among their foremost goals and with these in mind, they take each stage very seriously.

ESFJs relationships are bent on satisfying their partner's needs and creating understanding to build mutual support and respect. Letting them feel loved and appreciated provides them a gushing flow of self-esteem.

ESFJ Weaknesses

- Decisions that come out of ESFJs can be limited due to their concern over their friends, family or other relations. This results in using all means to satisfy other people or persons belonging to their own circle.

- As they place too much importance on socially acceptable actions or ideas they may appear or sound critical of the unconventional. They may push their own principles too hard in their effort to establish themselves as mainstream.

- ESFJs could, at times, be unwilling to dwell outside their own comfort zones, fearful of looking different from the rest. They may try to emulate what other people think is right which makes them deviate from who they really are.

- They have a need for constant appreciation and may fish for compliments if they don't see them coming. Compliments for them stand as reassurance for what they have done.

- ESFJs may overdo the quality of being selfless that they may neglect their needs without even noticing it. In their effort to help others solve their own challenges, their own issues may be left unsolved.

- They may manifest insecurities whenever things look uncertain or disorganized. They are organized individuals that is why they panic when stepping into a chaotic environment.

- Their set of moral codes is patterned to that of the community they are in and not coming from internal values.

The biggest challenge for the ESFJ personality is their problem concerning their own sensitivity. As long as there are criticisms, there will be hurt. They have to remember that hurt is a feeling and feelings are a part of life.

Because ESFJs indulge in social vigor and practical sense, careers they would find satisfying may revolve around using these qualities. ESFJs may work best in environments with predictable hierarchies and clear tasks. Routine work is not a problem for them; they will be too happy to do what is tasked.

Best Career Choices

Analytical careers are too dull for the ESFJ personality as they prefer human interaction and emotional feedback in order to gain satisfaction in their work. They are good working with teams and possess excellent skills in networking tasks.

Suggested Careers for ESFJs:

- Child care
- Nursing
- Teaching
- Social work

- Counseling

- Physician

- Receptionist

- Book keeping/Personal Accounting

- Office manager

ESFJ individuals are most compatible with ESFJ, ISFJ, ESTP and ISTP personality types.

Chapter 13
ENFP - The Inspirer

ENFPs are a truly free-spirited and like the ESFPs, they stand in the middle of social gatherings—giving life to the party. However, what they more excited about is not excitement that present itself but the connections, both social and emotional, that gatherings bring.

They are mainly characterized as energetic and compassionate; at the same time they are charming and independent. This type of personality comprises 7-8 % of the population—10% of them are women while men are around 6%.

Hobbies that ENFPs may be indulging in are:
- Writing
- Art appreciation
- Playing musical instruments
- Local theater performances
- Reading fictional books

Common Characteristics of the ENFPS

- ***Curious*** *towards new ideas*:   ENFPs will not hesitate to go outside of their comfort zones to experience new things or activities. They are highly-imaginative, open-minded and very curious about what more life can offer.

- *Observant*: ENFPs will try to notice every movement in ideas, actions or feelings as they believe that everything has a purpose and all ideas that fly in front of them are pieces that can solve puzzles.

- *Energetic and Enthusiastic*: These traits enable them to establish more social connections. These connections would translate later on as their resources for information or experiences. While they live in a world full of possibilities, they are also up to motivating and unendingly inspiring others.

- *Excel at Communication*: ENFPs are strong in people skills ad able to express their ideas clearly. They enjoy both small talk and meaningful conversations, and profoundly skillful at leading conversations towards subjects they desire to delve on using ways that appear natural or unforced.

- *Popular and Friendly*: They are persons who are approachable, exciting and interesting. This may have sprung from their being adaptable and spontaneous. Other people may see them as owning an altruistic spirit and empathic disposition.

- *Talented and Skilled*: These people may enter different careers in their lifetime because they are skilled at many things and fields. Their talent has a wide range that emanates from their innate creativity.

- *Great Interpersonal Skills*: They are interested in people as well as ideas. They place a great amount of importance on this aspect.

- *Happy People*: These happy individuals always love the company of people regardless of principles or desires. What makes them unhappy are mundane tasks or strict schedules.

Weak Points in ENFP

- *Poor on Practical Skills*: ENFPs have skills but do not include administration, upkeep and follow through; tasks that involve other people's help.

- *Get Stressed Easily* – These people are very sensitive, and care deeply about others' feelings which makes them burn out their energy. When the time comes that they have to do things on their own, their systems are bogged down and fail on their tasks.

- *Commit Serious Errors in Judgment*: They may arrive at the wrong conclusions once they apply their own perception even though they are good at intuitively perceiving truth in people or situation.

- ***Rely Much on Intuition*:** This is one of the errors that ENFPs have to be wary of. Relying too much on intuitions, assuming or anticipating too much on a friend's own motivations can make them misread signals. What would have been a simple approach could get complicated.

The ENFP in other Aspects

As Parents

What makes the ENFPs great as parents is their ability to share their sense of wonder on all things that are new and beautiful with their children and they do this as they grow. These individuals provide a good combination of love and overwhelming support alongside with unstructured environment that revolves in creativity and freedom.

They are able to provide time for playing with their kids and experimenting lots of things to add to their knowledge. They are known to encourage their children's interests and shift them towards things that may offer new knowledge.

This personality has the advantage of being open-minded and empathic. They are armed with the skill of spotting emotional problems or physical issues in their brood. But time and again, they may need the help of their partners in providing needed guidelines or discipline.

One fear that haunts ENFPs is the coming of age of their children where they would think of leaving home. They are afraid to lose their invested emotions and would start questioning themselves if they have been successful in raising them.

They can get lucky if they have raised them to be productive and independent citizens so as not be seen roaming around aimlessly and doing things that are against the society.

The ENFP Friends

ENFPs look at friendship as a chance to experience other perspectives. Being masters of attracting people, they instill prospective friendships with idealistic quality. They would go out of their way to know more people with reserved personalities.

They have this ability of keeping in tune with other personality groups as they take on the challenge of learning more about them in order to unravel the mystery that lie beneath people with different characteristics.

One would be too lucky to have ENFPs as friends as they are sincere and open-minded. These are people who understand well even their new acquaintances. They do appreciate and cherish the company of people who appreciate their kind of person. All the adventures and shared experiences they have with their friends are the stuff that make up the good life.

Relationships for ENFPs

ENFPs are up to sharing their bountiful ideas and eye-opening experiences in life with their partners. For them, a relationship is an exciting process of imagination and mutual exploration; an opportunity to connect with another psyche.

Relationships are taken seriously by the ENFPs who are known for being uninhibited and having unwavering devotion to people with whom they have committed their hearts to. They are persons who will do everything in their power to create a solid relationship by displaying sincerity and devotion.

Long distance relations never stood as a challenging situation for ENFP individuals as this gives them the chance to prove their loyalty and commitment; staying true despite the distance is a gauge for their sincerity towards the person they love.

On a sad note, people under this personality trait may easily fall apart after efforts to repair a broken relationship prove futile. They may seem reluctant to open up and commit again to another relationship. Nevertheless, if partnered with another person who feels comfortable and willing to dive into new experiences, they would come out from their shell.

On Careers

ENFP individuals may work best in situations that warrant flexibility and in environments that enable them to work with people and new ideas. They are geared towards becoming productive using little supervision, and working in jobs that takes their interest.

The ENFP personality type must take advantage of the strong qualities they have and use them to boost themselves further and nearer to where they are able or willing to go. However, the challenge they may face is not lack of skills or drive but the abundance of work that they are able to fit into.

Possible Careers for the ENFPs:

- Consultant
- Psychologist
- Entrepreneur
- Teacher
- Actor
- Counselor
- Politician
- Diplomat
- Writer or Journalist
- Television Reporter
- Artist
- Scientist
- Engineer
- Systems Analyst
- Computer Programmer

ENFP individuals are most compatible with fellow ENFPs, INFPs, ENTJs and INTJs.

Chapter 14
ENFJ - The Giver

The ENFJ personality is among the least common types (3%) found within the general population, most especially for men with 2% and women comprising 3%. Within the male population, it is the second rarest personality type. Hobbies that interest the ENFJs are:

- Reading
- Organizing Social Events
- The Arts
- Storytelling
- Writing
- Gourmet Cooking
- Listening to Music

This type of individuals possess a gift of expression that enables them to convey their feelings or emotions through communication. They are considered as warm, loyal, sensitive and outgoing.

Character Traits of the ENFJs

101

Persons who have ENFJ personality are focused on people and live in a world where there are lots of possibilities concerning people. Their minds are centered on supporting, understanding and encouraging other individuals; and these are besides bringing out the best in them. Simply put, they are highly capable of making things happen to earn satisfaction out of the deed.

People, in turn, love ENFJs. They are definitely fun to go along with and are typically honest and straight-forward. They exude self-confidence and own a variety of skills. By and large, they are bright, energetic and full of potential.

Many people consider the ENFJs as genuine and ultimately caring people who think that nothing could make their lives more meaningful than leading, motivating and uniting and motivating their team using their infectious enthusiasm.

ENFJs desire to double their efforts to maintain structure and would always wish to resolve ambiguity. People see them as fussy over the workplace and even at home.
ENFJs have clear-cut values and able to express their opinions which they're able to express clearly and direct to the point. However, they aim to be responsive, at the same time supportive of others. Whenever they are faced with conflict between values they hold firm and serving other people's necessity, they are likely to give importance to the latter.

Having strong communication and organizational skills, these people have the makings of great leaders or managers. They are likely to help each member of the group achieve their potential and could take steps in resolving their interpersonal conflicts. They will always strive to maintain harmony in all situations.

ENFJs are team players who listen and consider other people's opinions. They are, in every sense, reliable individuals who never let others down and be counted on whenever there is a need for help. They often land on leadership positions and admired by a wide majority due to their positive vision and strong personality that shines from within.

Weaknesses of the ENFJ Personality

- Tend towards being Overly-Idealistic: People belonging to the ENFJ personality type may be surprised to know that, through a circumstance or a simple misunderstanding, people would go against their adopted principles even though those principles are well-intentioned.

- Too Altruistic: ENFJ individuals tend to bury themselves with the hope of finding cure to other people's problems. In the long run, they can get burned and unable to help the next batch of people who may need their help.

- Varying Self-Esteem Level: ENFJs self-esteem may plummet as soon as they fail to reach their goal of helping others. They would ask how they fare in solving problems they face if just to extract their performance level in doing so.

- Reserved Extroverts: They have more reservations than other known extrovert personalities while having strong conviction on certain principles. They are more likely to hold back their pronouncements if doing so stands to interfere in extracting the best qualities of other people.

- Hate Dealing with Logic and Facts: They may be unhappy dealing with factual or logical ideas that are not concerning the human element. They may as well hate dealing with impersonal reasoning as they are unlikely to understand its merits.

- Dependent on Decision-making: An ENFJ whose Feeling side was not fully developed may have a hard time to make good with decision-making and may depend on others to perform the process.

- Tend to Overlook Merits of Current Situation: If it is their Intuition side that is underdeveloped, they may overlook possibilities which will push them to judge things basing them on previously set value systems or social mores regardless of the merits of the current situation.

Relationships for the ENFJs

ENFJ on Parenting Roles

Just as they are natural in the field of leadership, ENFJs make exceptional parents, who aim to strike a balance between providing encouragement and support to friends, partners and children. The ENFJ personality type dwell in a sea of empathy making them excel in parenting roles. They would help their children explore options and encourage them to follow their earnest desire. Helping the children grow to recognize and appreciate people's individuality is among their top priorities in raising their children.

They nurture them with strong values and ensure that these would be founded on from understanding and respect towards other people as well as themselves. As they inject them with these essential ingredients, however, they may succumb to become manipulative. On a good note, ENFJs would rely on their idealism and innate charm to make sure their young are ingrained with these lessons by heart.

Friendships as Seen by the ENFJs
ENFJs view friendship as an essential part of their life. People who have ENFJ personality take real pleasure in knowing other people and do not have any difficulty talking with personality types who have varied beliefs.

Their warmth and sincere optimism are felt by their friends, values that endear them so much to many others. ENFJs' goal is to be the best friend to almost everyone they know. They are very much capable of enhancing strengths, dreams and passions of their friends and nothing makes them satisfied than seeing them doing well whether at home, in relationships or in their chosen fields.

The joy that ENFJs gain from creating strong friendships is founded on the notion that establishing friendships do not end when they part ways for the time being. They look at this type of relationship purposeful and the bond they create is not easily shaken by just anything else.

ENFJ on Relationships

ENFJs require close and intimate type of relationships. This need makes them work on a lot of effort to create and maintain them. Their loyalty and trustworthiness would shine once they get involved in a relationship.

They take dating and relationships sincerely and may tend to select partners who is agreeable with long term plans. Their seriousness towards the bond is seen early on the dating stage wherein they would establish themselves as reliable and ideal future partners.

ENFJs employ a huge display of affection to provide their relationships the needed emotional medicine. They feel that they need to fulfill their promise of bringing happiness to their partners and seeing them satisfied with what they offer them is something to be contented about.

They are people who see to it that they are of help when it comes to assisting their partners in realizing their dream. They would support them in every which way to make their dreams come into fruition.

Many refer to the ENFJs as dependable lovers who are more interested in stability or routine rather than sexual spontaneity. ENFJ personality types believe true happiness can be possible if it is created mutually.

Best Profession Suggestions for ENFJs

People within the ENFJ personality circle focus towards careers that allow them to help other people. They belong to the driven and highly diverse group that can make them successful in the following fields:

- Counselor
- Teacher
- Psychologist
- Social Worker

- Human Resources manager
- Sales Representative
- Politician
- Coach
- Event Coordinator

Nevertheless they would avoid entering the following fields:
- Law Enforcement
- Military Service
- Emergency Response

People would find these individuals most compatible with INFJs, INTPs, ENFJs and ENTPs.

Chapter 15
ENTP - The Visionary

Another rare type of personality trait is the ENTP, wherein a person under this umbrella of characteristics is sometimes referred to as the visionary. Its rarity is seen in its statistics involving a handful 4% comprising the general population which accounts for 2.5% females and 5.5% males.

These intellectuals are fond of indulging in hobbies like writing, sports, computers and video games. They are also found highly interested in continuing education, cultural events and travelling from one place to another.

Characteristics of the ENTPs

Some researchers aver that ENTPs have a tendency to be analytical and independent; at times, impersonal in their dealings with people. They are the type whom many see as the most reluctant to follow a particular pattern. In short, they are not so much in favor of routines and may deviate from them from time to time.

Like the ENFPs, ENTPs have a profound understanding of the environment they are in and extremely accurate and fast in sizing up situations. These people are very adaptive when it comes to variety of tasks and their interests are abundant. Aside from the general characteristics they are known of, they are quite good at solving problems using sheer resourcefulness and intuition.

Although this personality type is more attracted to absorbing information rather than decision-making, they still count on using logical and rational approaches in order to reach conclusions. Well-developed traits found in ENTPs may cause them to lean towards being inventive, enterprising and having the skills of a visionary.

Other Attributes of ENTPs:

- Uncompromisingly Honest: ENTPs are hardliners when it comes to honesty. They would argue endlessly and if need be, step on other people's shoes if just to bring out the truth for what they believe in.

- Direct: They are people who would go direct to the point when they want to say something. They are not believers of beating around the bush to avoid adverse reactions from people who hear their pronouncements. This is also true with people who approach them to ask favors.

- Value Knowledge: They are up to spend more time in order to seek additional knowledge. They are skilled at using improvisations more so when the goal is to seek for a creative solution to a problem or concern.

- Clever: Of all the qualities of the ENTPs, this word is the thing that describes them best. They are able to juggle several ideas at the same time while doing another task. Their jokes are funny and at the same time very accurate and relevant.

- Excellent Brainstorming Skills: Mixing knowledge with originality is a skill that ENTPs are known to possess. They are people who are must-haves in brainstorming sessions.

The Lawyer in ENTPs

Objective and logical as they are, ENTPs are oftentimes called the lawyers among personality traits. Their Thinking quality is the aspect that is responsible for their being good at decision-making where everything is based on a list of rules and laws.

The ENTP personality type is also known by another name—the devil's advocate. Individuals under this trait just love to exercise mental sparring. They argue and make it known to everybody how they can get away with winning the argument for the fun of it.

They enjoy a broad display of their wit, wide knowledge base and the ability of connecting ideas to prove a point. This practice enables other people to enhance their sense of reasoning and to understand better opposing ideas brought to them by the ENTPs.

Weaknesses

Although there are several traits that make up the ENTP personality, weaknesses also come aplenty which is a sign that nobody is perfect. Here are some of them:

- ENTPs may lose their patience when dealing with people whom they consider as wrongheaded or those they think are unintelligent.

- They may seem to be unaware of the rest of the world as they are deeply indulged with their own thoughts.

- ENTPs think that follow through is more of a chore than a practical solution. An ENTP who has an underdeveloped Thinking side may jump from one idea to another and never finishing what they have previously started.

- ENTPS are prone to not noticing the personal aspect of situations. This potential problem may ensue when their logical strength isolates them from their own feelings and that of other people's.

- When under stress, ENTPs lose their capacity to generate possibilities and eventually become obsessed with trivial details; considering them as essential when in fact they are not.

Relationships

ENTPs love innovation and there is an unending stream gushing forth from their minds. This quality is also carried on through their relationships. To people belonging to this personality type, growth is a vital ingredient that long before they have found themselves dating partners, they have already thought of ways on how they can familiarize themselves with new things together so they can grow as a tandem.

This is an overwhelming process more so if their mates do not match up with their own personality. Unless they find someone who believes and shares their love for intellectual exploration, nothing positive would come out of the relationship.

Early on the dating period, ENTPs will test the limits of their partners when it comes to intellectual exploration; pushing boundaries or traditions and looking for spontaneity and open-mindedness. However, dating ENTP personalities is never a boring experience because of their creativity and natural enthusiasm. They are fond of surprises and they do this always to delight their partners using new ideas and other exciting experiences.

ENTPs are fantastic partners but their weaknesses would sometimes display their most obtrusive shortcoming which is emotional obliviousness. They are more likely to express emotional sensitivity which results to inability to discover that they have already hurt their partners.

Friendships in the eyes of the ENTP
ENTP personalities are respected because of their confidence, knowledge, sense of humor and vision. However, they often struggle in utilizing these positive qualities when it comes to friendships and romantic involvements.

They tend to bond closely with their loved ones. But while some of the may have the tendency to appear offhand, others are super demonstrative to the point of shocking their co-workers who have not seen them act like that.

ENTPs look forward to acquiring friends with similar temperament or interests such as theirs and remarkable at communicating with people with personality types other than ENTPs. Arguing is a natural tendency for them and when this happens, it means that they are already accustomed to the persons they are arguing with. The only persons whom they find hard to relate to are those who belong to the Analyst types.

Above all these, the ENTP personalities are not wanting for loyalty, emotional feedback or support from friends. They want directness in all aspects and never wish their friends to say yes even if they know that they are not treading the right trend of thought. They would want to hear those words only if they have earned it after a round of debate.

ENTP Parents
The heavy distaste for rules and regulations for the ENTPs is clear therefore they are expected to provide their children with the freedom they need in exploring life on their own. As the youngsters grow, their ENTP parents would encourage them to voice objections and to think independently.

They educate them in using options and look at them from a logical perspective in their effort to teach them impartiality. In this goal, ENTP parents need their partners' assistance to manage arguments and emotional outbursts.

In their effort to helping their offspring to develop into smart, honest and independent adults they need to communicate using rules that may be accessible to both sides. More likely, they would find utilizing some emotional expression tools in order to be more understandable towards their children as the best way to hurdle this challenge.

Careers for the ENTP Personality

What ENTPs love most is something that can help them flex their mental muscles. They like to develop new approaches, ideas and never run out of projects that would let them display their creativity. There are no limits to jobs they want to land on as long as the one they choose allows them to use their ingenuity.

Careers that ENTPs would enjoy are:
- Management
- Entrepreneurship
- Accountancy
- Human Resources
- Sales
- Analysis
- Research

This personality group is perfect when combined with the abilities of the INTP, fellow ENTP, ENFJ or INFJ personalities.

Chapter 16
ENTJ - The Executive

One of the least common of personality types is the ENTJ. This group stands as the rarest among women with 1% in the population and 3% found in men. Overall, this personality type comprises 2% of the general population.

It is said that this group is not content with jobs that do not demand the use of intuition because they are good at problem solving. Their hobbies range from attending social or sports events, engaging in competitive sports, and joining community groups where they take leadership positions. They may also become involved in leisure activities that helpful in their careers.

Common Characteristics of the ENTJs

Like other extraverts, the ENTJs are natural leaders and live in a world where there are many possibilities. ENTJs are focused on career and naturally fit well into the business world. They are quick at grasping complexities and able to come up with solutions in a flash.

They display tireless efforts on their job and capable of visualizing the future stand of any organization they are involved. They reserve no room for inefficiency and loathe the thought of repetitive errors. These reasons make them ideal corporate leaders.

People belonging to the ENTJ group are energized and highly stimulated as they interact with people. A challenging conversation is where ENTJs derive satisfaction and enjoyment. Besides the love for interaction, they give due respect to those who can stand up and argue persuasively if just to prove a point. But at times, people who are skilled at debates would experience self-doubt when facing ENTJs even in a normal debate encounter.

They are also known to be strategic thinkers as they take note of the essence of crisis management. They understand that solving momentary issues is just a temporal remedy. Therefore, they would take several steps in steering away from this practice in order to move on to fix the bigger issues which can provide better and grander results.

Being good at handling people happens because of their charisma and inspiring qualities. With these combined, they create people who are able to lead and invigorate others. These are also qualities that can make them pursue their ambitions and overcome the hurdles of tasks which need the help of others.

Challenges enliven the ENTJs. Provided with time and some resources, they will work hard to achieve their goal; may it be big or small. This makes up for their being brilliant entrepreneurs. They are very promising when it comes to long-range planning and able to execute strategic steps the precise way. Their strong determination may push them to involve others as they try to achieve impressive results for the sake of their goals.

However, this may result to self-aggrandizement and may alienate other people whom they have gripped in the process. By a stroke of luck, the populations should be thankful that this personality type only comprises a very small percentage; lest they are too many to handle, they could take advantage of the less shy and timid personalities that make up the entire humanity.

Weaknesses of the ENTJs

ENTJs can challenge other personalities as they are confrontational, intimidating and argumentative individuals. Their negative traits create their weaknesses and these are the following:

- They are people who have high standards and expect too much from others. They have a hard time listening to others because they think their intelligence is way above some of their peers.

- Due to their being unwary of other people's feelings, they are not good at expressing affection or sympathy which makes it hard for them to listen to what others feel.

- ENTJs are control freaks and always want to be in charge of things which may cause them to be overbearing, impatient and harsh. Their tempers would soar high during stressful situations.

- Due to their "unfeeling" nature, they may overlook praising others for their achievements, improvements or positive suggestions. They also find it hard to put themselves in someone else's shoes.

- ENTJs who have less developed Thinking side have difficulty in applying logic into their insights that equates to poor decisions and inconsistent in the decision-making process.

- ENTJ personalities think that emotional displays are a sign of weakness; thus, they are not at all in favor of showing others qualities they lack.

- They are ruthless when it comes to personal relationships as they tend to dominate their partners; this insensitivity breaks relationships and they are quite known for this reputation.

Relationships

People whom the ENTJs think deserve their respect are those who are their equals in terms of intellect and precision.

They regard romantic relationships as a serious business and are in favor of long term relationships. However, they can become overbearing parents or spouses.

Parenting Skills
ENTJs are determined to raise well-educated children.

Being focused on career and ambition gives them the tendency of being away from home and family most of the time. However, this does not make them bad parents. It only requires them to provide more personal liberty and emotional tact than what they are used to giving.

They hold the same high standards when it comes to parenting and like to be regarded as the role models of success. What they are less driven is establishing some moral values as they think cultivating intellect and independence are more important.

What challenges them when it comes to parenting is their weakness on the emotional tolerance aspect. If they are not good at strengthening this quality, dealing with adolescent children may be too hard for them to handle. Emotional expression is a certified form of communication which can help in minimizing conflicts that may constantly arise during encounters with their children.

Romance
The ENTJs look forward to have well-appointed homes and are devoted spouses who may work well with people who have strong characters and belong to the Thinking type. They regard dating as a gauge in finding the inner qualities that they want inside the person with whom they want to share their lifetime with.

They are dynamic when it comes to their sex life as they are into developing and trying new ways to get their partners satisfied with the experiences they put forth. Nevertheless, they have to remember that their partners do not only need satisfaction in bed but with emotional growth and support. They have to meet their mates halfway; thus, criticisms have to be accepted positively just as they want to hear praises.

Friendships
Friendships that were built on circumstances like projects or conventions are not the type ENTJ personalities are bound to treasure. They would seek friendly relations from people who share their own passions, know how to handle meaningful discussions and enjoy the idea of learning and development.

The more open-minded ENTJs recognize the fact they have to work on their emotional insensitivity in order to dismiss the thought that what their friendship brings is solely aimed towards personal growth. Being friends with the Diplomat groups can be rewarding because they share the same Intuitive trait which often results in accomplishments.

Aside from them, ENTJs are likely to befriend people under the Analyst category due to their passion for critical debate and logical approaches. Anybody who matches their brainstorming capacity and the ability to theorize will always find ENTJ individuals dedicated and honest.

Careers for the ENTJs

The ENTJs' drive and boldness are their best assets. No other personality type can be respected as a leader of a team or an organization aside from this personality type. They are one whole lot of reliable persons when it comes to careers as they have vision, determination and intelligence which could push them to overcome obstacles in order to completely push their ideas to fruition.

Possible Fields where ENTJs are found are:
- Corporate Executive Officer
- Entrepreneur
- Computer Consultant
- Organization Builder
- Judge
- Lawyer
- University Professors
- Administrators
- Business Administrators
- Managers

The ENTJ personality creates harmonious relationships with INTJs, ENFPs, INFPs and also ENTJs.

References:

1. http://en.wikipedia.org/wiki/ISTJ
2. http://myersbriggspersonalitytypes.tumblr.com/post/49234392873/istj-traits-the-duty-fulfillers
3. http://www.d.umn.edu/cehsp/studentaffairs/majorexploration/.../ISTJ.doc
4. http://similarminds.com/jung/istj.html
5. http://www.preludecharacteranalysis.com/types/istp/characteristics
6. http://www.preludecharacteranalysis.com/types/istp/work
7. http://www.istps.com/istp-careers/
8. http://www.quistic.com/personality-type/istp
9. http://www.red-doors.com/images/ISTP.pdf
10. http://welcometo-planethell.tumblr.com/post/39745204221/isfj-the-nurturer
11. https://www.smartlivingnetwork.com/personality-test/isfj
12. http://myersbriggspersonalitytypes.tumblr.com/post/49235688228/isfj-traits-the-nurturers
13. http://pstypes.blogspot.com/2009/04/myers-briggs-compatibility-part-2.html
14. http://www.humanmetrics.com/personality/ISFP
15. http://www.mypersonality.info/personality-types/isfp/
16. http://psychology.about.com/od/trait-theories-personality/a/isfp.htm
17. https://www.personalitymax.com/personality-types/isfp-artist
18. http://www.16personalities.com/infj-careers

19. http://www.truity.com/personality-type/infj
20. http://www.personalitypage.com/INFJ_rel.html
21. http://www.16personalities.com/infp-relationships-dating
22. http://www.16personalities.com/infp-strengths-and-weaknesses
23. http://www.truity.com/personality-type/infp
24. http://www.careertest.net/types/descriptions/intj.htm
25. http://www.personalitypage.com/INTJ.html
26. http://www.typelogic.com/intj.html
27. http://oddlydevelopedtypes.com/content/intj-parenthood
28. http://www.families.com/blog/the-mastermind-entailing-personality-type
29. http://www.16personalities.com/intp-personality
30. http://www.personalitypage.com/INTP.html
31. http://www.truity.com/personality-type/estp
32. http://www.true.co.za/downloads/mbti/estp.pdf
33. https://www.personalitypage.com/ESTP_rel.html
34. http://myersbriggspersonalitytypes.tumblr.com/post/49395302263/estp-traits-the-doers
35. http://psychology.about.com/od/trait-theories-personality/a/estp.htm
36. http://www.typefinder.com/personality-type/estj
37. http://www.personalitypage.com/ESTJ.html
38. http://www.keirsey.com/4temps/supervisor.asp
39. http://www.16personalities.com/estj-personality
40. http://www.true.co.za/downloads/mbti/estj.pdf
41. http://www.truity.com/personality-type/esfp
42. http://www.personalitypage.com/ESFP.html
43. http://www.typelogic.com/esfp.html
44. http://myersbriggspersonalitytypes.tumblr.com/post/49399479095/esfp-traits-the-performers
45. http://myersbriggspersonalitytypes.tumblr.com/post/49320157147/esfj-traits-the-caregivers

46. https://www.personalitypage.com/ESFJ.html
47. http://www.onlinepersonalitytests.org/mbti/esfj
48. http://www.true.co.za/downloads/mbti/esfj.pdf
49. http://myersbriggspersonalitytypes.tumblr.com/post/4
    9653035763/enfp-traits-the-inspirers
50. http://www.16personalities.com/enfp-personality
51. http://www.personalitypage.com/ENFP.html
52. http://www.truity.com/personality-type/enfp
53. http://psychology.about.com/od/trait-theories-
    personality/a/enfj.htm
54. http://www.truity.com/personality-type/enfj
55. http://www.16personalities.com/enfj-personality
56. http://www.personalitypage.com/ENFJ.html
57. http://www.personalitypage.com/ENTP.html
58. http://www.16personalities.com/entp-personality
59. http://www.typelogic.com/entp.html
60. http://myersbriggspersonalitytypes.tumblr.com/post/4
    9601106633/entp-traits-the-visionaries
61. http://www.true.co.za/downloads/mbti/entp.pdf
62. http://www.mypersonality.info/personality-
    types/population-gender/
63. http://www.mypersonality.info/personality-types/entj/
64. http://www.16personalities.com/entj-personality
65. http://www.personalitypage.com/ENTJ.html
66. http://myersbriggspersonalitytypes.tumblr.com/post/4
    9472805413/entj-traits-the-executives
67. http://www.true.co.za/downloads/mbti/entj.pdf
68. http://www.typefinder.com/personality-type/entj

Personality Types

ABOUT THE AUTHOR

Jane John-Nwankwo CPT, RN, MSN, PHN is a motivational speaker and published author of more than 30 books which include textbooks for healthcare training, fiction for entertainment, and motivational books.
Simply search
"Books by Jane John-Nwankwo"
On Amazon.com

Visit her website:
www.janejohn-nwankwo.com

Book Jane John-Nwankwo as your motivational speaker now at www.JaneJohn-Nwankwo.com

With more than 10 years as a professional speaker, Jane John-Nwankwo can hold any audience sitting straight on their chairs for any length of time! She is a seminar leader and a published author of more than 50 books including textbooks for healthcare training, fiction for entertainment, books for new entrepreneurs and motivational and inspirational books like the "It's in your hands" series.

She received her Masters of Science in Nursing from University of Phoenix, and is currently pursuing a PhD in Nursing Science from University of Phoenix. Her speaking interests include: Motivational speeches for new business owners, Motivational speeches for any category of people, Employee seminars, Students' Empowerment, Healthcare topics, Topics related to women and any Christian topic. Book a speaking appointment today and become a repeat customer because of 100% satisfaction.